STRINDBERG

STRINDBERG
by G. A. CAMPBELL

Great Lives

HASKELL HOUSE PUBLISHERS Lᴛᴅ.
Publishers of Scarce Scholarly Books
NEW YORK, N. Y. 10012
1971

First Published 1933

HASKELL HOUSE PUBLISHERS Ltd.
Publishers of Scarce Scholarly Books
280 LAFAYETTE STREET
NEW YORK. N. Y. 10012"

Library of Congress Catalog Card Number: 71-163501

Standard Book Number 8383-1320-5

Printed in the United States of America

CONTENTS

6 CONTENTS

CHRONOLOGY

1849....Born on the 22nd of January at Stockholm.

1867....Matriculated and entered Upsala University.

1868....Engaged as schoolmaster.

1869....Became an actor in Theatre Royal, Stockholm.

1870....*In Rome* produced in Stockholm.

1871....Received a pension from the King and returned to Upsala University.

1872....Royal pension stopped and Strindberg adopted journalism in Stockholm.

1874....Appointed assistant librarian in Royal Library.

1877....Married Siri von Essen, the divorced wife of Baron Wrangel.

1879....Made famous by the publication of *The Red Room.*

1883....Left Sweden and travelled in France, Italy, Germany, and Switzerland.

1884....Prosecuted in Stockholm for " writings injurious to morality and offensive to religion."

1885–
1894....Naturalistic period.

1888....Founded Scandinavian Theatre in Copenhagen.

1889....Returned to Stockholm.

1891....First marriage dissolved.

1892....Exhibition of Strindberg's pictures in Stockholm.

1893....Married Frida Uhl and visited England.

1894....Parted from second wife and engaged in scientific studies.

1895–
1898....Period of acute mental derangement.

1901....Married Harriet Bosse.

1904....Third marriage dissolved.

1907....Founded Strindberg Theatre in Stockholm.

1908....Took up residence in Blue Tower.

1910....Engaged to Fanny Falkner.

1912....Died on the 14th of May at Stockholm.

CHAPTER I

(1849-1867)

Parentage – earliest impressions fear and hunger – education – envious disposition – unhappy home life – quarrels with father and stepmother – training an iconoclast – humiliations of boyhood – religious perplexities – a strange correspondence – Strindberg at eighteen.

JOHANN AUGUST STRINDBERG was born in a house near the Clara Gate in Stockholm on the 22nd of January, 1849. The sixty years of his turbulent life were amazingly productive. He gave to Sweden a cycle of historical dramas unsurpassed in modern times ; he made a lasting impression on the European stage with his masterpieces of naturalism ; he introduced a new form into the theatre. But the theatre was only one of the activities of this tortured genius. He deserted the stage for years and poured out novels, essays, short stories, poems ; his autobiography is one of the most searching pieces of self-analysis in the world's literature. He composed music, and he threw himself with savage energy into painting ; he was a passionate reformer and a pioneer of Swedish Socialism. There are few subjects which did not engage his attention at some time.

Strindberg's whole life was one of revolt. He felt that he was born inopportunely, and that the world was unfair to him from his earliest years. He was the third child of his parents, Carl Oscar Strindberg and Ulrica Eleonora Norling, who had lived together for several years but had married only a few months previously. Strindberg refers contemptuously to his father as " the grocer," but actually Carl Oscar was a shipping agent and merchant who, after a long period of comparative prosperity in business, had been forced into bankruptcy shortly before August's birth. He was a man of culture and education, and prided himself on his noble family, which he traced back for centuries. His aristocratic instincts survived to the extent that, although at one poverty-stricken time parents and seven children were crowded into three rooms, he insisted that two servants should be added to the establishment. Nor would he permit his boots to be cleaned unless the servant wore gloves while doing so.

His relatives had objected to the irregular union with August's mother, not because it was irregular but because she was of the lower classes. Marriage made the break complete, for it was regarded as even more of a disgrace that a servant should bear the aristocratic name. She was the daughter of a poor tailor, and had met Strindberg's father while she was working as a barmaid in a Stockholm inn. Her marriage represented an ascent in the social scale, and she was grateful to her husband as the cause of her improved position, though she may not have loved him. The plebeian connection through his mother was a powerful factor in August Strindberg's life ; he felt " the blood of the slave " strong in him,

yet he could not identify himself wholly with the
working class. The two influences warred in
him, and traces of the struggle are found in many
of his books and plays. " I am the bondwoman's
son," he says, " of whom it was writ, ' Cast out
this bondwoman and her son ; for the son of the
bondwoman shall not be heir with the free
woman's son.' " He had an exaggerated need
for affection and was deeply attached to his
mother. " Born prematurely," he writes, " perhaps I am born incomplete." Throughout his
life, the mother remained his ideal.

August's first impressions in the ruined home
were of fear and hunger. An unwanted and
superfluous child, he learned that the highest duty
and virtue was to sit on a chair and be quiet.
Attempts to develop his individuality were dis-
couraged, and he claims that the foundation of
a weak character was laid in those early years of
repression. "Later on," he writes, in the first of his
autobiographical novels where he uses the third
person, "the cry was, ' What will people say?'
And thus his will was broken, so that he could never
be true to himself. Except on the few occasions
when he felt his energetic soul work independently
of his will, he was forced to rely on the wavering
opinions of others." Children lay on the ironing-
boards and chairs, children in the cradles and
beds, and the house was in a state of absolute
confusion. His father dared not introduce his
friends to such a home and would not accept

invitations that he could not return. His refuge was in music, of which he was passionately fond, and in the flowers which he cultivated in a window-box. He met the checks of life with resignation, and " God's will be done " was a phrase that August constantly heard on his father's lips.

Strindberg was a hypersensitive and self-conscious child who lived in perpetual fear of doing something wrong, and trembled at the least criticism. The slightest rebuke, or even the thought of having rendered himself liable to rebuke, would cause his tears to flow. An incident when he was eight years of age made a lasting impression on him. Some wine had disappeared and when August was asked whether he had drunk it, he blushed and shook in his nervousness. His father assumed from these indications that August was guilty and his mother urged him not to persist in his wicked denials but to tell the truth. Though innocent, he was regarded as the culprit and soundly thrashed. Another type of child would doubtless have forgotten the circumstance, but Strindberg recalled the injustice again and again. He refers to it in *The Dream Play*, and, in relating the incident in *The Son of a Servant*, he comments bitterly, " Family ! thou art the home of all social evil, a charitable refuge for indolent women, an anchorage for fathers, and a hell for children."

His mother took little interest in the children

who came regularly each year, and their up-
bringing was left to the servants. The Clara Lake,
near which the Strindberg house was situated,
had a reputation for suicides, and on quiet even-
ings, as the children sat by the lamp in the nursery, long, continuous cries would be heard.
Then, when the last cries of the drowning man
or woman had faded, the servants would tell the
children horrible stories of other suicides. Ghost
stories were also common in the nursery, and fear
and superstition were thus instilled into the
children. Strindberg suggests that since the
children of the rich and well-to-do are all brought
up by servants, the development of the race is
retarded. " It is an involuntary revenge which
they [the servants] take by inoculating our
children with superstitions which we have cast
out."

With returning prosperity, the family moved
to a six-roomed house in the Nortullsgata. The
Clara High School for children of the middle class
was a long distance from the new house, but it
was nevertheless decided that August should be
entered there when he was seven. In order to
reach the school in time, he had to rise at 6 a.m.
and start on a long walk without breakfast. He
stigmatises those days as a preparation for hell
and not for life.

A precocious child, he soon out-distanced his
classmates. Although his progress amply justified advancement to a higher form, the authorities

kept him back on account of his age, and August
rebelled against the decision. He knew himself
to be older than his schoolfellows in intelligence
and looked upon the delay in promoting him as
due solely to spite. The opportunity to leave
that school temporarily came shortly afterwards,
when, with his elder brothers, he was sent into
the country for the summer. Strindberg explains
that at this time he obeyed gladly and never
wished to put himself forward or be prominent,
so much of the slave was there in his nature. His
mother had served and obeyed in her youth and
" as a waitress had been polite to everyone."
He describes himself as being broad-shouldered,
with fair hair hanging over a forehead that was
sickly-looking, high, and prominent. Though
he read much and widely, he loved the open air ;
he was a good swimmer and a competent rider,
shot well, could sail a boat expertly, and enjoyed
hard physical exercise.

No sooner had he returned from the country
than he was again at loggerheads with the teachers
in the Clara High School, and his father decided
for the sake of peace to send him to the Jacob
School, which was attended by the poorer
children. Here Strindberg pursued his rebellious
way. He had assimilated so much that the slow
progress of the teachers irritated him, and if the
questions asked seemed unworthy of his knowledge, he simply refused to answer. Strindberg
was not amenable to discipline, and the position

became impossible for the teachers. They were unable to claim that he was dull, but, on the other hand, they could not allow their authority to be flouted and their methods to be challenged before the other scholars. A private school was found where August could pursue his studies by himself. He started on a varied course of reading, and laid the foundations of the encyclopædic knowledge which was to astonish everyone in later years.

His mother, worn out by the bearing of twelve children, died of phthisis when Strindberg was thirteen. He had tried to win her love but had never been her favourite, though she was proud of his learning and boasted of his quick brain. After her death, Strindberg was allowed for a time to do much as he liked. He had a mania for explaining and knowing everything, and was seized with the desire to surpass his brothers and sisters. One brother drew, so Strindberg set himself to learn to draw better. Other children could play some instrument, so Strindberg determined to master the piano in secret. He had not the patience to practise scales, but he learned to thump out pieces, and, while he never played well, his knowledge of musical technique was greater than that of anyone else in the house. Once he had mastered a subject – or believed that he had – that subject ceased to have any interest for him. During his walks in the country he had seen plants that he did not know, and he therefore studied all the varieties of plants in the

Stockholm flora. (When he found that all the plants in the neighbourhood were known to him, country rambles lost their interest !) He studied geology, formed an entomological collection, constructed a herbarium ; could distinguish the birds by their notes, their feathers, and their eggs. With much labour he made the inevitable attempt to solve the problem of perpetual motion.

In less than a year, Strindberg's father remarried. His second wife was the young housekeeper, and from the first Strindberg quarrelled with her. He accused his stepmother of beating his younger brothers and sisters and of cutting down food in the house. The older children did not support him in his charges, and Strindberg fought a lone and bitter battle against his father and stepmother. The latter took steps to revenge this annoying opposition. Although the financial position did not justify it, August was forced to economise by wearing unsuitable clothes ; his shirtsleeves reached only half way down his arms, and in the gymnasium in school he was ashamed to take off his jacket. The school cap which should have been his pride and joy disgraced him before his friends, for it was badly sewn – the only home-made cap to be found among the scholars. Poverty imposed as a measure of humiliation embittered those boyish years.

His criticisms brought other punishments upon him. He had to rise early and perform domestic

tasks before he went to school, and, when he complained that he had no time to keep up with his
studies, the sneering retort was made that he
boasted of being able to " learn so easily." What
wounded him even more deeply was that, although servants were not lacking in the house,
he had to act as nurse to his brother of seven.
He complains that it is a crime to confine him to
the society of children who are not on his intellectual level and has no doubt that his stepmother
tried to retard his development by this means.
At school, Strindberg was happy enough, for he
had his place and his rights ; but at home all
rights were denied him.   There he was like " an
edible vegetable cultivated for the use of the
family."

The learning in which he took such a soaring
pride was contemptuously brushed aside by his
stepmother. She was a pietist, and affected to
despise all worldly knowledge. When he was
present, she would make pointed remarks about
" higher things " compared with which book-
learning was a snare and a delusion   It would
not save people from hell ; what therefore was
the use of such knowledge ?   Once his stepmother and his eldest brother discussed with
grave approval a sermon they had heard in
church that morning and ignored Strindberg's
remarks as if he could not appreciate those veiled
mysteries. He retired to his room in fury and
wrote down the sermon from memory.   When
   Bs

he presented it to his stepmother, doubtless with a maddeningly superior air, she commented that "God's word should be written in the heart and not on paper." Strindberg, having no adequate retort to this thrust, violently assailed religion as a short cut for those destitute of culture.

He himself, however, became a very strict pietist. Primarily, he wanted to prove to his stepmother that he could be religious as well as learned, and he made himself insufferable at home by his strictness in religious exercises and by silently condemning such things as the Sunday picnics in which his stepmother and the rest of the family occasionally indulged. But, after many doubts and perplexities, religion became a real part of him, especially when he met a woman of thirty with whom he fell in love. At that time Strindberg was fifteen years old, and, not unnaturally, his family did not approve of the relationship, innocent though it was. A correspondence was opened between them and conducted in French. The subjects were sin, death, love, and scepticism. "Is Man's Life a Life of Sorrow?" is the title of one essay : in another, Strindberg discourses on the theme that there is no happiness without virtue and no virtue without religion.

The correspondence ceased and the acute religious phase passed when a school friend, whom he calls Fritz, introduced Strindberg to the amusements of the town. Wine, and the waitresses who

served it, engaged Strindberg's attention. Fritz
exercised a great influence on Strindberg's early
life. He proposed to go to the University, and
Strindberg determined to accompany him. His
father refused financial assistance, but Strindberg
believed that he could earn the necessary money
for himself. An opportunity came when a baron
engaged him as tutor for his children, and Strindberg saved the money he obtained in this uncon-
genial occupation. With his quarrelsome disposition, however, he did not retain the position
long, and returned to Stockholm from the baron's
country residence to study for his matriculation.

The examination was passed in May, 1867, and
Strindberg prepared for his first term at Upsala
University. He decided to be a professor, because " they could dress like scarecrows and
behave as they liked without losing respect."
His father presented him with a box of cigars
and exhorted him to help himself. An old servant
forced a loan of a pound on him, and from his
own work Strindberg had about five pounds. In
the autumn, he set out for the University with his
cigars and his six pounds.

Strindberg lays bare his child soul in the first
of his autobiographical novels, *The Son of a Servant*,
a document of much psychological interest and a
masterpiece of self-analysis. The child he presents is not lovable and is in many ways most
unattractive. The book pictures a clever, lonely,
supersensitive boy, who is envious, quarrelsome,

intolerably critical.   The circumstances of his
childhood were unfortunate, and Strindberg
never recovered from the torments and repression
of those early years.   It is a frank and shameless
description of the home that he gives, and he
does not spare himself or others.

Two of his sisters collaborated in a book entitled, *Strindbergs systrar berätta om barndomshemmet
och om bror August (Strindberg's Sisters Speak of their
Early Home and of their Brother August)*, in which
they complain that Strindberg has painted too
harsh a picture.   While, however, they protest
that he has misinterpreted certain incidents, on
the whole they confirm the main facts of *The Son
of a Servant.* August, they say, was a very difficult
child, always ready to contradict, always anxious
to argue about the most important and unimportant subjects.   Strindberg's sisters may not
have been unhappy in their youth, but, even if
the account given by them of those early years is
accepted, it is clear that to a boy of his character,
such a home must inevitably have been a humiliating prison.

CHAPTER II

(1867–1872)

STRINDBERG went to Upsala University as " the
ideal land." Not only was it the place where
" one could sing and get drunk, come home in-
toxicated and fight with the police without losing
one's reputation," but in it, he thought, his
doubts and perplexities would be settled and he
would learn what to do with his life. Upsala
came up to expectations so far as the relations
with the police were concerned ; but in everything else Strindberg was disappointed. He lived
with Fritz in a miserable room furnished only
with two beds, two chairs, and a cupboard. The
rent was a pound each per term ; the servant
supplied them at midday with their principal
meal for a little over seven shillings a month.
For breakfast they had milk and bread and
butter ; for supper, the same diet.

Strindberg soon found reason for criticism in
everything, and made himself thoroughly un-
popular by his comments. Fritz showed himself
more discreet. He had mapped out his career and
meant to be a lawyer. Dressed in his frock-coat,
he paid the customary visits to the professors

and created a favourable impression. Strindberg rejected the offer of the useful frock-coat and
refused to call on professors or anyone else. His
fierce pride would not permit him to pay court to
the authorities, as "to submit himself to his
superiors was in his mind synonymous with
grovelling."

The requirements of the degree examination
were a Latin essay, and he had no love for Latin.
Strindberg chose æsthetics and modern languages
as his chief subjects. Since his resources were
so limited, he attended only those lectures which
were free, but, after a single lecture on philosophy,
he calculated that it would take forty years to get
through the history of philosophy, and "that is
too long." He went to several of the lectures on
Shakespeare's *Henry VIII*, but decided that the
ten years it would take before the commentary
was finished were more than he could spare.

Strindberg could not afford to pay for the
private tuition which was regarded as a necessary
preliminary before a student could present himself for examination, and had no money to buy
books for individual study. He read such books
as he could borrow, but he realised that he was
making no progress. The extent of his accomplishment in the first term was the playing of the
B. cornet in the students' band. Fritz played the
trombone. The time had to be put in somehow.

Other students with no greater store and without half his abilities succeeded in making good

use of their time at the University, and Strindberg admits that the fault lay largely with himself.
He was shy and retiring, and would not mix with
others from whom he might have learned. Apart
from the depressing conditions of his life, however, the principal cause of his failure was that he
lacked the spirit of enterprise. At school he had
been told what to do and had done it – at least,
sometimes ; even at the private school his studies
had been directed to a certain extent. At the
University, however, the students were left to
themselves, and it appeared to be a matter of indifference to the authorities whether anyone
worked or not. He had no initiative and was
overcome with lethargy and despair.

The six pounds had disappeared before the end
of the first term and Strindberg returned home to
Stockholm in a penniless state at the end of 1867.
His failure depressed him and the sarcastic remarks of his friends infuriated him. " Are you a
complete scholar now ? " they enquired, and he
was made to feel an impostor and boaster. Since
it was winter, he could not even wear the white
cap of the student. A post as an elementary
school teacher was offered to him, and, although
such a position was considered a disgrace for a
student, Strindberg was glad to accept it. The
salary was a pound a week, which seemed to him
wealth, but the post was in the Clara School to
which he had gone as a boy. Any other school
might have been bearable, but to serve in his old

school seemed to him like reverting to the past ;
again and again in his work he condemns his
characters to re-live former experiences as the
worst of punishments.

The only consolation was that he would be able
to buy books and study for his degree examination.   Neither then nor later was Strindberg able
to live within his income.   The pound that had
appeared so much did not permit of carouses, of
fine clothes, of rich food, of the purchase of books.
But the fact that he had a regular income made
it easy for him to borrow, and Strindberg took full
advantage of the chance.   He had started to
drink heavily, and throughout most of his life he
was a slave to alcohol.

Temporary relief from his financial difficulties
came when he found private pupils, but he made
himself ill in trying to accomplish too much.   A
Jewish doctor, Axel Lamm, rescued Strindberg
from this life.   He recognised Strindberg's quality,
appreciated his problems, and made the proposal
that Strindberg should study medicine, giving up
all his teaching except that of the two Lamm boys.
To help the suffering appeared to Strindberg the
highest aim in life, and he entered on his new
studies and duties with characteristic enthusiasm.
Life as a member of the Lamm family was pleasant.   Interesting and cultured people were frequent visitors, and Strindberg was treated as an
equal ; for the first time in his life he had
access to a good and extensive library, and the

theatre was only a stone's throw from the house.

At this period it seemed to him that he had separated himself from all working-class influences and had definitely won for himself a place among the cultured. But an incident convinced him that he was still the son of a servant in feeling and that his life was bound up with that of the people. There was a general desire to erect a statue of Charles XII of Sweden, and all classes of the community contributed to the fund. Stands were erected for the unveiling ceremony, but so unskilfully had they been put up that only a few favoured people would be able to see the unveiling. While dinner was in progress at Dr. Lamm's house, shouting was heard outside on the evening before the ceremony. Then came the tramping of horses and the sound of weapons. The prima donna of the Italian Opera Company, who was among Dr. Lamm's guests, asked the cause, and a professor replied that it was only the mob misbehaving itself.

Strindberg jumped up from the table and ran from the house. "The mob!" he repeated. "They were his mother's former associates, his own schoolfellows and afterwards his pupils," says Strindberg in the second of his autobiographical novels *The Growth of a Soul*, which is also written in the third person. "They formed the dark background against which the company he had just quitted stood out like a brilliant picture. He felt as though he were a deserter and had done wrong in working his way up. But he must get above if he were to do anything for those below." Before he could take any part in the riot, however, he was firmly escorted back to the doctor's house. On the day of the unveiling, the mob again showed its dissatisfaction, and Strindberg threw in his lot with the rioters. He found a policeman in the act of arresting a rioter and sprang forward with the demand that the prisoner be released. " Who are you ? " the policeman asked irresolutely. " I am the devil," shouted Strindberg, " and if you don't let him go, I'll take you." The policeman thought that Strindberg was more worthy of arrest after such a statement, but a stone knocked off the policeman's hat and gave the opportunity to both prisoners to escape.

After this incident, Strindberg was deeply discontented with his position as a member of a rich household. His early enthusiasm for medicine waned, and when the doctor, to show him how great was the need for skilled treatment, took the student to his surgery, Strindberg found his thoughts wandering to the poets he had read, to the plays he had seen, and he decided that medicine was a " dirty profession." He was still resolved, however, to take his degree at Upsala, and in the spring of 1869 he presented himself for examination in chemistry. Friends pointed out that as he had not studied in the professor's laboratory he would be plucked, but Strindberg felt confident of his qualifications. "We shall see," he replied, "whether knowledge does not tell." In this instance, apparently, it did not, and Strindberg retired dejectedly.

As he was passing the Carolina Library in Up-sala, he heard people laughing at the long rows of books which could be seen from the street. Strindberg recognised them as actors and actresses from the Stockholm theatre ; and " they laughed – the men and women laughed at the books." Strindberg's faith in learning had gone with his failure to pass his examination, and there and then he determined to be one of those lucky per-sons who can spread culture without the aid of books. Throughout the summer he studied act-ing, and presented himself in the autumn to the Theatre Academy with a demand for an engage-ment.

The interview with the director of the Academy is typical of Strindberg's attitude. He wanted to play Karl Moor, the leading rôle in Schiller's *The Robbers*, and brushed aside all other parts as unworthy of him. When the director referred to a part in a popular success, Strindberg pointed out that after the triumph obtained by the last actor in the same part he dared not risk a com-parison ! Nor would he consider a minor rôle, offering as his reason that the rôle must be great enough to sustain him. " In a minor rôle," he explained to the director, " one must be a great artist in order to attract attention." But with a principal rôle, the part itself would sustain him. These views did not commend themselves to the management, and, after a period of training, he received an invitation to play a part in Björnson's *Mary Stuart* which consisted only of the line, " The Lords have sent a messenger with a challenge to the Earl of Bothwell." Strindberg, however, was not satisfied until he had been cast for a leading part, and he complained so consistently that he got his way. The performance was a total failure. Strindberg himself realised his deficiencies and went home to commit suicide. The opium pill he had kept for an emergency failed to act, and a friend took him out to drink his sorrows away. That was the last of Strindberg's acting. When the next performance was due, he was cast as the prompter !

Strindberg never regretted the time spent as an actor. The knowledge gained in that capacity proved valuable throughout his life, and especially when he came to found his own theatre. Doubtless he would have turned to the stage even if he had never acted – his grandfather, Zacharias Strindberg, had been a dramatist – but the connection with the Theatre Royal led him to dramatic composition earlier than might otherwise have been the case. On the day after his failure in the leading rôle, scenes formed themselves before his eyes as he lay miserably brooding over his plight. As the scenes unrolled, Strindberg discovered that a comedy in two acts was ready to be written.

In four days the piece was finished, and it seemed
to him as though " the years of pain were over, as
though a tumour had been cut out." That same
evening he sat down to write a note to a friend,
and was amazed to see that he had written a four-
page letter in rhyme. He had often tried to write
verse and the failure to do so had been one of his
greatest griefs. Now " it seemed to him like the
working of the Holy Spirit. It was not till this
moment that he noticed in himself the so-called
creative power of the artist."

The piece, *An Anniversary Present,* was sent to
the Theatre Royal, but met with rejection. A
tragedy written round his own religious experiences had the same treatment, but the director
was impressed and advised Strindberg to take a
degree and adopt authorship as a career. The
thought of returning to the University, " where
men's souls grew rotten from overproduction of
thought," was distasteful, but Strindberg resolved
to follow the advice. A small legacy from his
mother, extracted with great difficulty from his
father, made it possible to become a student at
Upsala once more, but while there he founded a
club, drank heavily, and did everything except
study. He wrote furiously, and at last a one-act
play, *In Rome,* was accepted for production at the
Theatre Royal in Stockholm. The acceptance
of a play at the age of twenty-one seemed an
adequate recompense for all his troubles and
privations, and Strindberg attended the first

performance in the autumn of 1870 with high
hopes.   But the play on the stage made him
deeply ashamed : he felt that it was unworthy of
him, and, although certain of the comments were
severe, he had to admit that the critics were
justified in attacking the piece.

University life after the production of his play
was still more distasteful to Strindberg, and he
did not remain long in Upsala.   He returned to
Stockholm, and studied æsthetics by himself, and,
when he had completed his thesis, presented it at
the University.   The professor returned it with
the remark that the subject was more suitable for
a woman's magazine of the popular type than for
a thesis.   Strindberg, always ready to accept a
challenge, cast doubt on the professor's knowledge
of the subject, assailed the University teaching,
and put forward suggestions as to how it might be
improved !   The professor pushed him out of the
room, and even Strindberg was not surprised to
learn that he had failed again.

Although he determined never to return to the
University, he became a student again in the
autumn.   It was greatly against his inclination,
but from every side he was told that he could
never succeed as a writer unless he had taken his
degree.   He arrived at Upsala with exactly one
shilling in his possession and had to live on his
friends.   His room, rented with borrowed money,
had a camp bed, without sheets or pillows, and
practically nothing else.   He could rarely afford

to buy fuel and had to study in bed – except on washing-day in the house. The chimney passed through and partially heated Strindberg's room.

In the midst of his troubles, he had the gratification of having another play accepted for production at the Theatre Royal. The piece, *The Outlaw*, had no greater success than the former play, and the critics were again unkind. One member of the audience had, however, been impressed. The play dealt with the Vikings, and Charles XV, then on the throne of Sweden, was a man of artistic temperament keenly interested in such work. He made enquiries regarding the author, and Strindberg's presence at Court was commanded. It seemed too good to be true, and, suspecting a hoax, Strindberg sought definite confirmation before he set off to wait on the King. Charles was genial and laudatory, but more important to Strindberg was the fact that the King offered him financial assistance on hearing the student's plight – and Strindberg did not hesitate to mention that his father, now a prosperous shipping agent, had limited his contribution to a box of cigars. The King promised him a pension of fifty pounds a year, and Strindberg left the palace joyously with the first instalment.

His return to Upsala was in the nature of a triumph. He was the King's protégé, and as such life was made easier for him so far as external things were concerned : now he was envied where before he had been despised. Strindberg felt that the pension imposed obligations on him, and he set himself to serious study. He won minor successes, and nothing appeared to stand in the way of his graduation. His attempts to take a degree were, however, doomed to failure. His conduct had become more and more unreasonable, and culminated in an incident at the newly formed æsthetic club. Professor Nyblom had praised Dante, and Strindberg thereupon attacked him. Whatever the professor approved, Strindberg claimed as a proof of failure in the poet – and concluded by describing *The Divine Comedy* as an obsolete and verbose pamphlet! Strindberg's performance was characterised as " shameful " and he was advised to rest. That was impossible for him : he turned from books to painting, and, locked in his room, began to paint furiously. Then a dreadful suspicion came to him : Had he gone mad? He heard two acquaintances discussing him, and it seemed that they spoke as if they doubted his sanity. Awful terrors assailed Strindberg, and he wrote to a private asylum asking to be received for treatment. The director of the asylum, having found out the facts of the case, relieved Strindberg of the fears that possessed him but gave a warning as to his future conduct.

Strindberg was undecided what to do, but circumstances imposed a decision on him. After the first instalment of twelve pounds the King's treasurer sent no further remittance, and, in reply to Strindberg's enquiry, wrote that Charles had never intended to award a pension but merely to make a gift on one occasion. A further sum was forwarded, with the intimation that it would be the last. Shortly afterwards, in 1872, the King died, and Strindberg never learned definitely the cause of the withdrawal of the pension. Ten years later, he heard as an explanation of the King's disfavour that he was reported to have composed a lampoon on his patron. Whatever the real cause, Strindberg was secretly glad to be his own master again. The obligations imposed by the King's pension had chafed.

He left Upsala University without regrets, " abandoning dreams and the past to live in reality and the present."

CHAPTER III

(1872–1876)

STRINDBERG was, as usual, penniless when he arrived in Stockholm, but, rather than seek his father's aid, he borrowed money to rent a room in one of the poorest quarters of the town. The desire to write had gone, and Strindberg did not seek to recapture his inspiration. " The little letters huddled together on the paper were dead and could not express his mind so plainly and spontaneously " as painting. He chose gloomy subjects for his pictures : generally he painted the sea, " with the coast in the foreground, some gnarled pine-trees, a couple of rocky islets in the distance, and a white painted buoy." His friends were sought among a group of artists who dreamt of enormous canvases which no studio could house. One of the group wished to paint the sea not merely as a level, but with such a wide horizon that the roundness of the world would be indicated !

Hunger alone made Strindberg give up his painting and look for other work. Characteristically, he refused to consider an application to a

daily newspaper to which he had contributed in
his student days, but found a position on a small
evening paper of pronounced radical tendencies.
He was deputed to write art criticism, and added
to his meagre salary by turning out novelettes
and articles for a women's journal. The brief
career of the radical newspaper ended ingloriously,
and Strindberg gave up his connection with the
women's journal when he found that the payment
was less than that of a domestic servant. He
retired to a little island near Stockholm and set to
work on his first great historical drama. The
fishermen were generous to him, but often he
could not write for wondering whether he would
be able to get food for the next day. In the play,
as in most of his work, Strindberg dramatises his
own experiences.

Despite the sordid circumstances in which he
lived, *Master Olof*, under the title of *The Heretic*,
was written in two months. It had only been
undertaken after a long period of hard reading.
He had studied Buckle's *History of Civilisation in
England*, and gathered from it that the masses
alone were important ; he had been impressed
with de Tocqueville's *Democracy in America*, from
which he concluded that the masses were the
worst of masters ; the views of Sören Kierke-
gaard, the individualist Danish philosopher, had
remained strong in him since his early student
days in Upsala, and he had been affected by
the pessimism of Von Hartmann. Shakespeare,

however, was the most decisive influence on Strindberg in the writing of *Master Olof*. As a boy he
had read Shakespeare in Swedish and been very
critical. Nothing in the plays had appeared to
him worthy of the praise that came from every
quarter ; but when he could read Shakespeare
in English, Strindberg changed his opinion.
Although, however, the influence of Shakespeare
– especially *Julius Cæsar* – is obvious in *Master
Olof*, the full measure of Strindberg's appreciation
did not come for several years yet.

Master Olof was written in prose and treated
the characters realistically. Strindberg knew
that it was his best work, and rushed back to
Stockholm to lay it before the Theatre Royal.
The play was rejected, though the management
offered to reconsider it if certain alterations were
made. But the alterations proposed meant an
entirely different work. In the first place, prose
was to give place to verse ; then the realistic
treatment was to be modified ; and the historical
personages were to be dealt with in kindlier
fashion and not dissected by Strindberg's searching
hand.

The rejection of the play by which he had hoped
to establish himself plunged Strindberg into the
deepest dejection. He was twenty-three and
still uncertain of his own gifts. The time when
he had felt sure of his ability to conquer the world
had been succeeded by doubt of his powers. In
his disappointment, Strindberg turned against

everything that he had previously supported.
" He had only one opinion – that everything was
wrong ; only one conviction – that nothing could
for the present be done to make things better."
But he had to live, and acting again appealed to
him as the solution to his difficulties. A visit was
made – on borrowed money – to a Gothenburg
theatre, and Strindberg was actually offered an
engagement at ninety pounds per annum. The
theatre would not, however, open for two months,
and Strindberg's impatient soul could not wait
so long. The fact that a management had been
willing to give him an engagement restored his
faith in himself to some extent. He gave up his
solitude and consorted with artists, writers,
teachers, and journalists in a little club which met
in a room with red furniture in Bern's restaurant.
Nothing was sacred to the members ; they were
rudely and coarsely critical of everything and
everyone, including themselves, and Strindberg
delighted in the brutality of the attacks on society
as it was ordered.

A project to establish a paper devoted to insur-
ance matters, then a burning question, was carried
out, with Strindberg as editor ; but the paper
soon came to grief. Strindberg escaped to his
island, where he tried to drown himself because
he could not pay his debts, but had a love-affair
instead. The discovery that the woman was unfaithful to him drove Strindberg back to Stockholm in a state of collapse and disillusionment.

He appealed to his father for refuge, and lived at home for a short period. Then restlessness seized him again and Strindberg borrowed his fare to Sandham. Here he dwelt with pilots and coastguardsmen and was physically and mentally restored. " I know you have written plays," a friend said to him at this time, " but aren't you going to do anything *useful* ? " Strindberg surveyed his life and found that he had no " useful " accomplishment by which he could live. There was a telegraph station at Sandham, and Strindberg decided that he would earn his living as a telegraphist. He had learned enough telegraphy to send the weather telegrams when, as so often happened with Strindberg, an unforeseen offer came to him. He had sent some letters to the Stockholm *Daily News*, and the editor was so impressed with their descriptive power that he invited Strindberg to join the staff.

Strindberg had visions of moving the world by his influence as a writer on an important journal, but he soon discovered that the *Daily News* was different from a radical newspaper. He was expected to be discreet, and discretion was not in Strindberg's character. One of his duties was to report debates in Parliament, but he was so disrespectful to the honourable members that another job had to be found for him. He was given reviewing, and, *à propos* of a religious publication, wrote that the publishers had undertaken a heavy responsibility by disseminating such untruths.

So Strindberg was turned loose on the theatre. Theatres had not been kind to him and he had old scores to pay off. As dramatic critic, he paid them off with interest. A theatrical company suffering under his sarcastic remarks threatened to horsewhip him ; the editor complained that the *Daily News* was losing its reputation for impartiality ; and Strindberg thought it time to remove himself.

He resigned from his post, and a period of starvation followed. He was ill from lack of food, despised as a failure by everyone. The club in Bern's which had afforded him so much interest was now dissolved, and those members whom he still saw were suspicious of a man who had thrown away so many golden opportunities. Even when he had money, he hesitated to go into a restaurant in case he should meet anyone who knew of his reverses. He felt that he was being pointed out as a man who had been found wanting in everything, as one for whom there was no place in the world. Death or lunacy, he writes, would have been welcome. Anything to free himself from the purgatory in which he was living.

Over a year had passed since he had said good-bye to Upsala with such high hopes, and during that time he had never known repose. No job had lasted more than a few weeks, and he had always been hedged in by debts. But now came to him a much coveted position which set him again on the path of respectability. He had at first refused to act on the advice of a friend to apply for a post in the Royal Library of Stockholm, for he had no influence, no University degree, and his life had been irregular. Two of his plays had, however, been produced in the Theatre Royal ; another, *Sinking Hellas*, had been awarded a medal by the Royal Academy ; and he had been a protégé of the late King. These things could not be overlooked, and Strindberg was appointed assistant librarian.

The work in the Royal Library was light, but Strindberg could never take life easily. He performed tasks outside the range of his work, and, when his ability had been recognised, he obtained permission to catalogue the Chinese manuscripts in the library. It was an undertaking which an experienced Chinese scholar might have hesitated to tackle, and Strindberg knew no Chinese. In a year he had learned enough of the language to enable him to start the work, and in a few months he presented the catalogue to the library authorities. He was recognised as the sinologue of the library, and entered into correspondence with other sinologues in various parts of the world.

Strindberg had become really interested in the culture of China. He decided to make practical use of his knowledge, and the result was a monograph entitled *Sweden's Relations with China*. Membership of learned societies rewarded his work ; the Imperial Russian Geographical Society presented him with a medal, and he had

hopes of receiving a Russian order. His acquaintances respected him as a man who had succeeded;
his achievement was now of the respectable kind,
and he was regarded as a man who had sown his
wild oats and returned to take an honoured place
in society. One hardly recognises the irrational
Strindberg in this conventional librarian. He
remarks of himself that he had " succeeded in
contracting a healthy idiocy which seriously
threatened to kill all intelligence ! "

As might have been anticipated from Strindberg's previous experience, when the inevitable
break with convention came, it was on a grand
scale. He was twenty-six at the time of meeting
with Siri von Essen. She had been married for
a number of years to the Baron Wrangel, the
bearer of a distinguished name in Sweden and a
man of consequence. He was a captain in the
Guards, a competent officer, and from the first
was very friendly to the young author, whom he
recognised as his intellectual superior.

Siri von Essen, Baroness Wrangel, was a Finn,
and a woman of great charm and beauty. No
other woman ever influenced Strindberg so
greatly ; no other woman was ever loved by him
so deeply. She attracted him at the first meeting.
" The girlish appearance and baby face of the
Baroness – who must have been at least twenty-
five years of age – surprised me," he writes. " She
looked like a schoolgirl ; her little face was
framed by roguish curls, golden as a cornfield on

which the sun is shining ; she had the shoulders
of a princess and a supple, willowy figure ; the
way in which she bowed her head expressed at
the same time candour, respect, and superiority."

She had a girl of three, and Strindberg saw
mother and daughter in the rôle of Madonna and
Child. The acquaintance developed ; the Baron
approved of him and Strindberg was allowed
the freedom of the house. He was " royal secretary " in the library, had a reputation of sorts as
a playwright, and was a contributor to important,
if financially unremunerative, magazines. His
income was not large and he was deep in debt,
but he contrived to live in good style. Strindberg is described at this time as full of fun and
play. The tawny hair no longer fell over his
lofty forehead, but was brushed straight up in a
somewhat theatrical manner. He had blue eyes,
bold and penetrating, but his face was spoiled by
a small, weak mouth – " a serpent's mouth," it
has been called.

The Baroness was keenly interested in the
theatre, and that was a bond between her and
Strindberg. She talked of the confining life of the
home and wanted to adopt acting as a profession,
but the wife of a Guards officer could not be
allowed to appear on the stage. Strindberg
writes that their attraction for each other in the
early days was that " she was a soul in torment, a
voice unable to make itself heard, just like myself."
The Baron was a few years older than his wife,

and, although constantly complaining of poverty, he managed, the Baroness told Strindberg, to maintain two expensive mistresses. When Strindberg came on the scene, the Baron's new love was a cousin, and Strindberg acted the part of keeping the Baroness occupied while the Baron pursued his love-making.

Whether the Baron saw how things were shaping between his wife and Strindberg is uncertain. It seems clear, at any rate, that Baron Wrangel did not much care, and that in the circumstances the marriage was bound to break up even without Strindberg's intervention. On the whole, however, the Baron probably did not see Strindberg as a danger to, or as a deliverer from, the marriage bond. He remained on very friendly terms with the young author, and Strindberg reciprocated the feeling, though occasionally he felt that no real friendship was possible between him as the son of a servant and the Baron as the representative of a noble family. In conversation the Baron mentioned casually that he had been with the Guards when in 1868 they had charged the mob at the unveiling of the statue in Stockholm. Strindberg had a vivid recollection of that riot in which he had taken part, and his revolutionary instincts rose against the Baron as an aristocrat.

But such incidents were very rare. Strindberg, apart from his love for Siri, was happy to be on familiar terms in the house of an aristocrat, and could not repress a feeling of astonishment that he, a plebeian, should have climbed so high in the social scale. When the Baroness left Stockholm for a visit to Finland, Strindberg and the Baron felt desolated and consoled each other. Both wrote to her, and Strindberg handed over his letter for inspection. " I never read other people's letters," said the Baron. " And I," Strindberg replied stiffly, " never write to another man's wife without the man's full knowledge of the correspondence."

Strindberg's feelings underwent violent changes. Sometimes he felt madly in love with her and would pay homage to the Baroness's picture as to a goddess. At other times he talked of her " wrists and ankles exquisitely beautiful " and indulged in sensuous fancies. In the large attic he occupied, Strindberg " arranged the flower-pots in a semicircle and placed against them the picture of the Baroness with the lamplight falling upon it. In the portrait she was represented as a young mother with somewhat severe but deliciously pure features, her delicate head crowned with a wealth of golden hair." But there were occasions when she inspired only disgust, and he would shrink from her as something unclean. He fled from her flower-encircled portrait to a drunken orgy. After a quarrel, he ridiculed her before his friends. " I surpassed myself in heaping insults on the head of my Madonna. It was the morbid result of my

unsatisfied longing. . . . My messmates, acquainted
with love in its lowest form only, listened eagerly
to my vile denunciations of a lady of rank who
was utterly beyond them."

Strindberg had made one unsuccessful attempt
to flee from the Baroness and now he determined
to try again to escape from her influence. He
announced his intention of going to Paris, and
embarked on a boat for Havre. But the ship had
no sooner left harbour than he began to feel
lonely and tell himself that there was no purpose
in a visit to Paris. He made up his mind to go
ashore on the next day. "With the spring of a
tiger," he writes, "I bounded up the stairs and
stood before the captain. ' Put me ashore or I
shall go mad.' " A place was found for him in
the pilot's cutter, and immediately Strindberg
was on dry land – in a resort where he had passed
happy days with the Baroness – shame overwhelmed him. He called himself criminal for
having such a love, irresponsible for lacking the
power to leave it behind him. Only one thing
could fit in with his mood. He must make a
grand renunciation. Since he could not live
without Siri, he would die – but not without her
to see him pass away. Strindberg conceived a
melodramatic scheme of dying from pneumonia !
He would linger till she came to his side. "I
should have to be in bed for some time. I could
see her again and kiss her hand in saying good-
bye – for ever." He chose a cigar and drank

an absinthe and then went out to contract pneumonia, not forgetting, however, to book a room
in which he could die comfortably on his return.

Nothing could be urged against Strindberg on
the ground of thoroughness. He swam far into
the sea and, on reaching the shore again, sat
naked till he shivered with the cold. Then,
leaving his clothes below, he climbed an alder-
tree and clung to it through an October gale.
It was a satisfaction to him as he dressed to feel
that he had put his early death beyond all doubt.
He wired to the Baron and retired to his room
to depart this life. As a last precaution, he took
an overdose of a sleeping-draught.

In the morning both the Baron and Baroness
arrived, full of concern for their friend. Strindberg received them in a state of almost rudely
insulting health. The sleeping-draught had pro-
cured him a good night's sleep and the exposure
to the gale had merely given him a huge appe-
tite !

Strindberg struggled against his love no longer.
He returned to Stockholm, and the confession of
his love was made to the Baroness shortly afterwards. She could not have been unaware of his
feelings, though she professed to be surprised, and
admitted her love for him. The attic, " that
temple of adoration, became the abode of their
guilty passion."

CHAPTER IV

(1877–1883)

Marries Siri von Essen – child born – growing reputation as a
journalist – wins fame with *The Red Room* – influence of
Dickens – Strindberg as satirist – anti-feminism – hatred of
Henrik Ibsen – quarrels with Siri – departure from Sweden.

SIRI VON ESSEN excused her infidelity to the Baron
by citing his infidelities, but Strindberg insisted
that the husband should know the position. At
first the Baron seemed prepared to let Siri go
her own way while remaining his wife, provided
that his name was not publicly disgraced ; but
scandal broke out and, pressed by his relatives,
the Baron decided to seek a divorce on the ground
of desertion. In order to provide justification for
the technical plea of desertion, Siri retired to
Copenhagen for a few weeks, and the Baron
obtained a divorce, with the custody of the child.

The divorce was granted in the spring of 1876,
and the way was clear for Strindberg and Siri
to marry. But she valued her freedom, and Strindberg was not anxious to undertake the responsibilities of marriage with a woman to whom he
could not be constant. They continued as lovers :
" Everything was now permitted, but temptation
had diminished." The repulsion which he had
felt towards Siri at intervals throughout their
friendship became stronger as time passed, and
the occasions of it more frequent. He could not

47

live without her, yet he despised himself for wanting a woman in whom there were so many things
that aroused disgust in him. He combined, as is
not unusual in men of great ability, extreme
sensuality with equally extreme puritanism. All
his life he fought against his sensuality, with little
success ; and the partner for the time being in
his sensual adventures – and there were many
partners – was included in the disgust which
overwhelmed him afterwards.

He hated the publicity of the divorce, and his
repulsion from Siri grew to such an extent that
he made another effort to escape from Stockholm.
A friend had received an unexpected legacy, and
invited Strindberg to spend it with him in Paris.
Strindberg was a good companion for a few weeks
of reckless living and he was particularly glad of a
good excuse to leave Siri at this time. He did not
turn back on the way, as he had done on the
previous occasion. His sojourn in Paris, however,
was brought to a sudden end, for Siri wrote that
she was about to become the mother of his child,
and Strindberg hurried back to her side. It was
in the rôle of mother that he had first worshipped
Siri, and he rejoiced that she should play that
part again – this time, to his child. On the
30th of December, 1877, the marriage took
place.

For thirteen years she was to colour nearly all
his work. The story of that tragic marriage is told
by Strindberg in *The Confession of a Fool*, which

he himself called a terrible book. It is a shameless and heartless piece of work. There are in it some passages of much beauty, but equally there are pages of bestiality and sheer drivel. Strindberg says that he never intended the book to be published at all, but that in a time of intolerable financial embarrassment he was forced to sell it for publication in France. (Strindberg wrote the book in a vigorous but not strictly grammatical French.) Against his express wish, parts of it were serialised in a Swedish newspaper, but its publication in book form in his own country was prohibited until after the death of his wife and himself. Strindberg admits that the book should never have been written, and states that he keenly regretted the mad idea of relating the story of his marriage. It is very doubtful, however, whether he felt so repentant as he makes out, and, indeed, whether he realised the unpardonable nature of the book. He had no reticence whatever about his most intimate affairs, and regarded others as similarly constituted in this respect. *The Confession of a Fool* gives Strindberg's story of his first marriage, and can be shown to be inaccurate in several instances – the book, in fact, is full of inconsistencies. The eldest daughter of Strindberg and Siri, Karin Smirnoff, has written a study, *Strindbergs första hustru* (*Strindberg's First Wife*), which presents the other side.

Strindberg entered on marriage with Siri with a deep sense of the responsibilities involved. In
Ds

addition to his salary from the Royal Library, he earned an appreciable income from his journalistic activities. He was becoming known as an independent thinker and a writer on whom editors could rely for interesting matter, and commissions flowed in upon him. His capacity for work was astonishing. He wrote with great speed in a fresh style which was occasionally ungrammatical but was always clear. His brain teemed with ideas, and he could not transfer them to paper speedily enough. He rarely read over his articles, and he kept strictly to a time-table. In the morning he decided his work for the day, thought over his subjects during his daily walk, and took pride in finishing at the time he had fixed. Throughout his writing career he rarely failed to keep closely to his schedule. His vitality was amazing and his rapid production was the despair of the critics. Day after day, he could write without a stop for hours on end until he had completed a play or a novel, and then immediately start on a new work.

The first child of his marriage with Siri, born early in 1878, was a sickly girl who survived only two days. Another daughter came in the following year, and Strindberg was overjoyed. He loved all children, and was a devoted father, though he had his own ideas of the part they should be allowed to play in the life of a man of genius. His domestic life was apparently happy at this time. Siri had resumed the rôle of

Madonna, and the child seemed to Strindberg the paragon of children.

In other things, Strindberg was not so satisfied. His journalistic articles met with a ready sale and had an appreciative public, but his books fell stillborn from the printing-press. In the year of his marriage he had published a description of his life in Upsala under the title *From Fjardingen and Swartbäcken*, and the critics had torn the stories to pieces ; a new version of his play, *Master Olof*, written in verse, was simply ignored when it appeared.

Strindberg might have forgiven the critics for their attacks on his Upsala book, but he could never excuse indifference to the best play he had written till then. Choosing as his motto Voltaire's dictum, " Rien n'est si désagréable que d'être pendu obscurément," he castigated Stockholm society in *The Red Room*, which appeared in 1879. The room with the red furniture in which the artists' and writers' club had met in Bern's restaurant had given him his title, and he had no lack of knowledge of the capital's weak spots. *The Red Room* is a realistic novel which describes the career of Arvid Falk (Strindberg), a young journalist who comes to Stockholm with high ideals and noble ambitions and is quickly disillusioned with the condition of affairs that he finds. Such a book could not be overlooked. It became a popular success, and Strindberg, at the age of thirty, found his name on everyone's lips.

The critics ridiculed him for his grammatical errors and accused him of imitating Zola (whose work at that time was unknown to him), but the people were unaffected by the criticism and bought the book. Strindberg says that he was influenced by Dickens, especially *Pickwick Papers*, in writing *The Red Room*, but he had nothing of Dickens's heartiness and broad humour. Dickens was one of his favourite authors throughout his life. He wrote that he wept over *A Christmas Carol*, which, at one of the darkest moments of his career, revived his faith in human nature, and when, years later, he was asked to state his favourite author, he bracketed Dickens with Hugo.

The Red Room, with its exposures of the hypocrisy and sharp dealing of the rich, was used by the Socialists as propaganda. The young writers rallied round in defence of a book which broke away from the academic tradition in literature. Strindberg's name became a battle-cry. He was now on the crest of the wave, and further successes followed. In the following year *The Secret of the Guild* was published, and met with acceptance. Although not a play of great intrinsic interest, it is of importance as showing Strindberg's development. It is the bridge that leads to the naturalism of 1886, and there are in it traces of the symbolism which was to mark Strindberg's work in his last phase.

Then *Master Olof* was, after five revisions,

scheduled for production, and the first performance was given on the anniversary of the
author's marriage. The play had forty-seven
performances, which represented decisive popularity. The relief which Strindberg experienced
at his acceptance as a significant dramatist and
novelist has left traces in his work of this period.
Lucky Peter's Travels, written joyously in fourteen
days, is the work of a happy man. The fantasy is
reminiscent of Ibsen's *Peer Gynt*, but was intended
as a play for children. It has remained one of
the most popular of Strindberg's works. Rarely
again did he exhibit the genial humour of *Lucky
Peter's Travels*. The third act especially is rich
comedy of a kind we do not associate with the
author of the most morbid plays ever written.

Popularity was short-lived. There came a re-
action, and when Strindberg published *The
Swedish People*, the hero became a degraded
blackguard. His clear vision had seen things
which he believed wrong and he did not hesitate
to attack them. His mission in life, he says, was
to be the fault-finder and the destroyer, and he
was vitriolic in his outbursts. *The Swedish People*
(1882) was a searching enquiry into Swedish institutions, and the reception given to the book
seems to have decided Strindberg to demonstrate
what he could really do in the way of abuse. His
reply to the criticisms was *The New Kingdom*, a
book of essays published in the same year. This
is Strindberg at his most slashing, careless of

everything and everybody. Not only did he attack the sacred institutions – including the throne and the army – but he used his satirical pen to trounce public personages against whom he had a real or imagined grievance. The book is a highly reprehensible production from a moral point of view, but it is extremely witty, and the comparison of Strindberg with Swift as a satirist rests for some of its justification on *The New Kingdom.*

Quarrels with his wife added to Strindberg's perplexities at this time. He had wished Siri to write, since she was anxious to " express herself," and had collaborated with her in a charming children's book. She had, however, retained her love for the theatre, and, while the stage had been closed to her as the wife of Baron Wrangel, she was able to choose her own career after the divorce. Before she married Strindberg Siri was given a trial at the Theatre Royal in Stockholm and hailed as an actress of outstanding abilities.

Strindberg had written to her, " You are not born only to bring children into the world," and told her that the marriage would be a union of equal partners, each with absolute liberty of choice. After marriage, he changed his mind and wished his wife to give up the theatre. He declares that she could not act – he refers to her as having insolent gestures and bad manners and as being boastful and overbearing on the stage – and that she had obtained her engagement only because the scandal of the divorce had made her notorious. Siri, however, was an actress of merit, though not of the first rank, and while Strindberg may have favoured her withdrawal from the theatre, he does not appear to have expressed any strong views on the subject. It was not until the fourth year of their marriage that her independent life seems to have perplexed Strindberg at all keenly. By that time he was famous and had an income adequate to support his wife and family without the salary she earned at the theatre.

The cause of Strindberg's active opposition to his wife's independent career is to be found in the work of the Norwegians, Ibsen and Björnson, especially the former's *A Doll's House*. Norwegian thought dominated Swedish intellectual life, and was in Strindberg's opinion a baneful influence ; he felt that his own country should not accept ideas merely because they were exported from Norway. While a student at Upsala, he had protested that Swedish literature was in bondage to the neighbouring land, and claimed that the genius of the two countries was quite different. " The Norwegian cannot laugh," he writes. " He is hard, implacable."

Henrik Ibsen's name was great in Sweden, and Strindberg recognised him as his only rival. *A Doll's House* received an eager welcome from the feminists, who used it as propaganda for their movement, while Björnson also threw the weight of his authority – by no means inconsiderable – on the side of the women's movement. Strindberg was not in sympathy with the movement, but his frantic hatred of the " equality delusion " and of the " emancipated woman " did not develop for some years yet.

Karin Smirnoff suggests that her father was merely being contrary in his opposition, and that he had no real feeling in the matter one way or another. But the charge of insincerity cannot be maintained against Strindberg in respect of his anti-feminist writings. It is doubtless true that he was glad to find himself as an opponent of Ibsen. " The famous Norwegian blue-stocking " is Strindberg's description for him. His hatred of Ibsen took an acute form in later years, and he believed that Ibsen despised him. The contrary was, however, the case, for, although Ibsen admitted his dislike for Strindberg, he acknowledged Strindberg's genius. A visitor found a portrait of Strindberg in Ibsen's study and expressed surprise at its presence in view of Strindberg's slighting comments. " I don't like him," Ibsen is reported to have replied, " but I can't write a line unless that portrait is there. He will be greater than I." Various versions of the story have been told, but all agree that Ibsen pointed to the portrait of Strindberg as that of a writer who was, or would be, greater than himself.

Strindberg claims that he always believed that

men and women should be equal in duties and responsibilities, and that in his youth he had considered it absurd that boys should give up their places to girls and quite unjustified that girls should have to do mending for boys. On one occasion he invited the boys to let the girls carry their own shawls at a picnic, and thus have real equality ! But while a student he had collaborated with Dr. Lamm in an article opposing the proposal that women should be allowed to become doctors. The article had been published with alterations which made it appear to support instead of oppose the proposal. " Women behind it," had been Strindberg's comment.

Equality which involved women in competition with men in the labour market seemed to Strindberg monstrous. A woman should be a mother and a housewife, her domain the home. Siri's independent existence was at loggerheads with the theories that began to possess him in 1883, and he made an earnest appeal to her to surrender her career. Siri was not so enamoured of the stage as at first, but she refused to give it up altogether. The quarrels which started with the question of her career ranged from her dog to the food which was served in the house. One row of which Strindberg gives an account involved both.

He was not a pronounced animal-lover, but, while he had no violent objection to other animals, he could not suffer dogs in his presence. Siri was much attached to her poodle, which Strindberg

found objectionable.   One day he was served with
a totally inadequate meal, and found the servant
in the kitchen engaged in cooking an appetising
supper that he would have welcomed.   But the
food was for the dog !   Strindberg complained
that he was treated worse than the loathsome
animal, and Siri responded that he had no reason
to object, since she paid for the dog's food from
her own earnings.   " And what do I pay for ? "
Strindberg raged madly.   Another quarrel arose
over the consumption in a single month of five-
hundred bottles of beer !

Rumours of the dissensions in the Strindberg
home got about in Stockholm – hints were thrown
out in *The Newest Kingdom*, which was published
as a counterblast to Strindberg's *The New
Kingdom* – and Strindberg determined to leave his
native country.   He published a historical study
which was favourably received, but he followed
it in 1883 by *Poems in Verse and Prose*, which again
brought him into conflict with literary Sweden.
Siri was induced to accompany him – with dog ;
and Strindberg departed gladly from the capital
where he had been raised from insignificance to
the pedestal of a prophet and then, after a brief
period of triumph, cast down with contempt as a
mad iconoclast.

CHAPTER V

(1883–1888)

Anti-feminism – prosecuted for impiety – triumph in Stockholm –
success and failure – utilitarianism – social reformer –
obsessed with hatred of women – fear of matriarchy –
believes himself persecuted – naturalistic masterpieces –
power of suggestion – vampires and man-eaters – theory of
superman – *Hedda Gabler*.

STRINDBERG's wanderings took him to France,
Switzerland, Italy, and Germany. Paris was
congenial to him, and among artists and writers
he felt that he had found an appreciative society.
But a sudden disgust of the artificiality of town
life seized him, and he left hurriedly at the beginning of 1884. A trip which he made to Italy had
an important influence on him. He served as
special correspondent for the Stockholm *Daily
News*, and in that capacity dived deeply into Italian
life. The Socialist theories which had never
been far from his mind became prominent again
in his work, and Strindberg felt that on him, a
member of the proletariat and endowed with
authority through his genius, lay the duty of
exposing the defects in a system which made
slaves of millions.

He settled in Switzerland to write a book which
would be at once propaganda for Socialism and a
protest against the " unhealthy cult of woman-
worship." In the *pension* were thirty women,
" idle, gossiping, pretentious, longing for pleasure."
Most of them were English, and Strindberg

noticed that when their husbands joined them, weary with work in cities, the men had to fetch and carry. " There were learned ladies who left the *Saturday Review* behind them on chairs," writes Strindberg ; " there were literary ladies, young ladies, beautiful ladies. . . . He asked himself, ' Whom do these parasites and their children live on ? ' The husband sat in a dark office far away in London ; the husband was far away with a detachment in Tonkin ; the husband was at work in his office in Paris ; the husband had gone on a business trip to Australia."

Strindberg felt that this was a condition of affairs that ought to be pointed out to the world, and in 1884 he published *Married*. He had thought that he knew the lengths to which abuse could go, but Strindberg was aghast at the storm which broke out on the appearance of the book in Sweden. In *Married*, he tells the stories of a number of marriages ; some of them are humorous, some vulgar, some tragic, some cynical. One description of a marriage is " like a little liaison I once had in the old days. There is only one difference – this one is duller and costs more." He wrote a story as a reply to Ibsen's *A Doll's House*, and used the same title. In the story, husband and wife have lived very happily for six years. While he is absent a friend introduces her to Ibsen's *A Doll's House*, and the wife is brought " to realise that she is only a doll." She writes to her husband, " How earthly, how material our love has been," but

Strindberg brings about a happv ending to the
troubles that then arise.

The most famous story in this starkly realistic
book is " The Reward of Virtue." It is of a
young man who has lived a life of sexual repression. An older and over-sexed woman marries
him out of hand, and the youth dies exhausted
from the sexual excess imposed upon him by his
wife. Such a story was regarded as indecent by
the authorities, and there were other tales equally
objectionable, in their opinion. It cannot be
said that Strindberg was rabidly anti-feminist
at this time, but the feminist movement regarded
him as such and joined the moralists in the on-
slaught on the author. Strindberg claimed that
in *Married* he praised women who undertook their
proper duty in the home, and in the preface to
the book he has sketched out a programme by
which the legitimate rights of women would in
his opinion be met.

He believed that only under Socialism could
the inequalities disappear. He favoured votes
for women, and advocated that a woman should
retain her own name after marriage and not lose
her identity in that of her husband : he urged
co-education, and wished boys and girls to learn
only reading, writing, and arithmetic, a knowledge of the laws of the country and of the duties
of citizenship, together with one foreign language.
" In accordance with the law of nature," he
writes, " every citizen will have to earn his own

living as nature ordains." The influence of
Rousseau is obvious in the preface.

The man who put forward such a programme
cannot be justly accused of lack of sympathy with
woman's rights, but Strindberg had no patience
with the view that women were weak and clinging
mortals eternally overreached by men. He was
at once branded as a woman-hater by those who
did not appreciate his plea for a new basis in
marriage. The moralists and feminists gained their
point and the book was suppressed by the police.
Proceedings were commenced against the publisher, but the charge was not one of immorality,
as had been anticipated. The Queen of Sweden
is said to have considered the book indecent, but
the authorities felt doubtful of succeeding on such
a charge. In one of his stories, however, Strindberg
had drawn on a boyish experience in the country.
There he had assisted a sexton to prepare the
wafers for communion, and in *Married* he referred
to the market value of the wafers in a stupid way.
The author was on that score regarded as having
written matter offensive to the established religion
of Sweden, and the publisher was charged with
disseminating the impious work.

The blow stunned Strindberg. He wrote from
Geneva to the police, but his letter was ignored.
A second letter brought the suggestion that he
should return and stand trial. He was uncertain
what course to pursue : his wife urged him not
to go, and he was told that conviction would be

certain. The son of the publisher rushed to Geneva and put the position before the author. Strindberg felt that he could not allow the publisher to bear the brunt of the attack intended for himself, and, on a promise that the proceedings against the publisher would be withdrawn if the author appeared, Strindberg set out for Stockholm.

He lost his nerve badly during the journey. People came to the train at the stations *en route*, and their gloomy summing up of the prospects of his reaching a prison cell made him weep bitterly. Two years was the term imposed by statute, and Strindberg felt that his chances of escaping the maximum sentence were slight. In Stockholm, however, he had a wonderful reception. The young writers who had rallied to his support on the publication of *The Red Room*, but had deserted him later, now renewed their allegiance ; the Socialists turned out in force to welcome their most distinguished member ; and there was the inevitable crowd ready to cheer anyone who was " agin the Government." His progress to the hotel was a triumphal one ; a theatre put on one of his plays for a special performance – the chosen piece was *Lucky Peter* ! – and when Strindberg appeared he was cheered to the echo.

The case was eagerly followed by all Sweden, and fierce passion was aroused. The charge failed, and Strindberg was escorted back to his hotel by a joyous mob. A medal was struck to commemorate the great victory, and a banquet was given in his honour. Strindberg was hailed as the leader for whom young Sweden had waited, but he had neither the qualities nor the desire to take part in public life, and he distrusted the crowd which "cheers to-day and boos to-morrow." He fled back to Switzerland and his books.

The prosecution scarred Strindberg's soul. He knew that his motives had been pure, and the suggestion made in the Government newspapers that he was a purveyor of pornographic literature aroused him to a pitch almost of madness. In his prosecution he saw the hand of the feminists, and he began to imagine that they were pursuing him, seeking to wreck his life. "Cherchez la femme!" he writes when he hears that a manuscript has gone astray. The feminists are behind everything, plotting to remove their most powerful antagonist secretly since they have failed in a direct attack. He subscribes to anti-feminist journals, rarely fails to add a warning against women to his letters at this time, and is full of the most awful forebodings of the fate of the world. The men are asleep, he cries, while the women are getting ready to enslave them. He discovers that there is a widespread plan to found a matriarchy, and believes it is his sacred duty to call his own sex to defend themselves from female domination.

The following year, however, he managed temporarily to overcome this obsession, and brought out one of his finest books, *Real Utopias*. He had come to the conclusion that art should be utilitarian. "As you perhaps know," he writes to a friend in 1885, "I am a disciple of Rousseau and Tolstoi." John Stuart Mill was another influence at this period, and Georg Brandes he had always read though not always understood. Strindberg feared the beautiful in art as tending to veil the truth, but he was too much of an artist to adopt the severe utilitarianism that he advocated. *Real Utopias* presents in a series of short stories some of the more obvious evils of the world and shows Strindberg's tenderness for the poor and unfortunate. His solution is along Socialist lines, and for the Socialist Party in Sweden the book became the text of many speeches. But Strindberg resisted all attempts to bring him into the hurly-burly of affairs. One experience of leadership had been enough.

The constructive suggestions of *Real Utopias* were forgotten and Strindberg was again regarded as merely an insensate destroyer when the second part of *Married* appeared in 1886. The first part was unjustly characterised as the outpourings of a woman-hater, but there was no doubt of the attitude of the writer of the sequel. Strindberg brought to this book a fierce determination to expose the women whom he believed intended to make men their slaves ; he would be merciless to those who had persecuted him ; they had asked for battle, and he would give it to them. Strindberg was convinced that women were naturally inferior, not only mentally and morally,

Es

but biologically. And when the inferior seeks to dominate, then the higher must whip the lower back to its place. The book is the production of a man suffering from overwrought nerves and possessed with an unreasoning hatred of women.

He had in the same year worked at the autobiography of his early years. Strindberg believed that autobiography came nearest to truth and that it was destined to replace the novel for that reason. He wrote to his friends and relatives for letters and documents, and tried by their assistance to recapture the past. But he was writing at the age of thirty-seven of things that had happened in his youth, and he does not succeed in avoiding occasional inaccuracies. Despite the distortions, however, the work remains one of the great autobiographies of the world, franker than that of Rousseau or Tolstoi or Goethe, unsurpassed as an analysis of the mental growth of a man of genius.

His fame as a European dramatist was established by the four plays that he wrote in 1886 and the following year, plays of impeccable logic and masterly construction. Strindberg had written nothing for the theatre since 1882, for the failure to secure production for *Master Olof* when first written had left him with a permanent grievance against theatre managers ; but now he felt that he could express himself only in drama and that the theatre needed him. The public was surfeited with the pieces which had no contact with reality, and Strindberg considered that he was called upon to " present life as it is." He had no patience with what he called " little naturalism." " Merely to sketch a piece of nature in a natural manner is not true naturalism," he writes. " The true naturalism seeks out the crises in life where the great conflicts occur." It loves to see " what cannot be seen every day, rejoices in the battle of elemental powers, whether they be called love or hatred or social revolt," and "cares not whether a subject be beautiful or ugly, if only it is great."

" I am going to write two plays," he tells a friend in 1886. " After all, the theatre is my real vocation." The first of these plays, *Comrades*, shows Strindberg striving after the naturalistic form, but not wholly achieving it. The theme is of an unsexed woman who tries to take the fame of a man and live in the light of his renown. Bertha and Axel are " comrades " who live together and pursue their artistic career in apparent friendly rivalry. Both have sent pictures for exhibition and they discuss the chances of their success. She asks him to use his influence with a member of the judging committee, and when he refuses she taunts him with being afraid that she will succeed where he fails. There is great excitement among all their friends when she announces that her picture is to be hung while his has been rejected. It is the triumph of the female over the male, and Bertha flaunts her superiority. To add to his humiliation, she arranges that the rejected picture shall be delivered in the studio when a party is in progress, but she has plotted her own undoing. The numbers have been changed, and the returned picture is seen to be her own and not Axel's. The incident has revealed to him Bertha's real nature as a mental parasite and marauder (the play was originally entitled *Marauders*), and he leaves her. He can find his comrades in the cafés. At home, he wants a wife.

The play pleased Strindberg at first, and he sent it to his publisher with the request that a theatre be found for its production " in order to show up the feminists." His publisher neither liked nor approved the piece, but a Copenhagen theatre offered to produce it. A happy ending was suggested, with Axel showing manly forgiveness to the erring partner whom he had taught a salutary lesson, but Strindberg refused to permit the alteration. By that time he had lost his faith in the play and wrote that it was full of imperfections. His next play, *The Father*, was to show him as a master of æsthetic naturalism, though even yet he did not feel that he had achieved the form completely.

The Father was written at the beginning of 1887, when Strindberg was developing his theory of the superman. He had regarded the world as consisting of two classes, aristocrats by birth and plebeians, and he had taken the part of the

plebeians ; but now he brushed aside that division as unimportant and conceived the two
classes as those of superior and those of inferior
intellect. By birth he is the " son of a servant " ;
by genius he belongs to the ruling class. The
feminists and all others who seek to oppose him
are jealous of his superiority of brain.

His theory of utilitarianism in art was cast
aside. As always with Strindberg, he destroys the
gods he has worshipped before he feels able to
swear allegiance to the new. The fact that he
has renounced old ideals proves that they are
wrong, and Strindberg never passes on without
attacking the theories that he advocated and now
rejects. So now he pours contempt on those who
think that art should be utilitarian. No longer,
he says, is he interested in social and political
reforms ; the only conflicts which are worth
while to him are psychological. In a German
newpaper he writes that he is not a prophet and
has no wish to be a martyr. The honours which
the aristocrats by birth offer him are no temptation, and the plea that he should lead the proletariat falls on deaf ears, since the artist has
more to do than support a party. Nor does he
see himself in the rôle of conscious educator. He
is simply a searcher after truth, and, like a chemist,
is indifferent whether or not his analysis reveals
arsenic. He condemns the practice of introducing numerous characters and of changing the
scene. The ideal should be absolute simplicity

in staging, the fewest possible number of characters, and a psychological struggle presented with
complete detachment on the part of the author.

Everything else was advancing in the world ;
why then should not the art of the murderer ?
To use a knife or poison to remove an unwanted
person was a crude and antiquated way, and in
these days of clever police such a murder would
soon be discovered. More subtle means were
required, and Strindberg saw in suggestion the
modern method of getting rid of unnecessary
persons – especially men who stood in the way of
wives who wished to dominate ! His correspondence and articles are full of references at this time
to what can be accomplished by the power of
suggestion. He reads a book in which a woman
" suggests " that her enemy should seek death
by hanging, and Strindberg immediately writes
on the awful possibilities that are thereby opened
up. He finds that Shakespeare had no other aim
in view in *Othello* than that of showing the power
of suggestion as practised by Iago. As we shall
see, Strindberg was in later years to believe that
by suggestion he could cause injury to those who
opposed him.

" I am really obsessed by the feminist question,"
Strindberg wrote at the beginning of 1887, when
he was engaged on *The Father*, and the play is the
work of an obsessed man. It is again the antagon-
ism of the sexes in ghastly form. The father is an
intellectual and cultured cavalry captain married

to Laura, an inhuman monster who plans his
ruin. He wishes to decide the education of the
child, Bertha, and is opposed to his wife's ideas
on the subject. A struggle commences between
them, and both husband and wife realise that it can
only end in the death of one or the other. Laura
advances the possibility that the captain is not the
father of Bertha, and the thought poisons him. For
what father, asks Strindberg, can ever be quite sure?

At the end of the second act, Laura says :
" Now at last you have fulfilled your part as the
– unfortunately – necessary father and supporter !
You are no longer needed, and you can go ! You
can go, now that you have realised that my
intellect is as strong as my will – since you won't
stay and acknowledge it ! "

The captain throws a lamp at Laura as the
curtain falls. Strindberg says that the idea of the
lamp came from England. He understood it was a
common habit among English husbands, and when
he considered English wives he was not surprised !

As the play proceeds, Laura, much the inferior
in intellect, shows herself vastly the superior in
ingenuity. She poisons everyone against her
husband and spreads rumours about his sanity.
The perplexity over the parentage of the child
works in the captain's mind, and, by a devilish
power of suggestion, Laura drives her husband
to madness and death. Throughout, the captain
is shown as a somewhat weak character, but he
explains that he was brought up by women and

so has been brought up weak! Ever since his
birth – and his mother did not want him to be
born – he has been at the mercy of women, and
in the play it is his old nurse who performs the
final act which conquers him. Laura is the
egotistical, ignoble, horrible woman whom Strindberg sees as bent on subjugating men.

The Father was attacked for its morbidity on
production in Copenhagen, and Strindberg referred to the attacks in the preface to his next play,
Lady Julia. " A short time ago," he writes, " my
tragedy, *The Father*, was criticised for its sadness
– as if one wanted cheerful tragedies. There is a
clamorous insistence on the joy of life, and managers are sending out requests for farces, as if the
joy of life consisted in being idiotic and in portraying all men as sufferers from St. Vitus's dance or
congenital idiocy. Personally, I find the joy of
life in its tense and cruel struggles, and my
enjoyment lies in getting to know something, in
getting to learn something."

Lady Julia was attacked even more fiercely than
The Father on its production. Edvard Brandes
had suggested that Strindberg should study the
repertory of the Théâtre Libre established in
Paris by Antoine, and Strindberg had found in
the plays produced there support for his belief
that the number of characters should be reduced
to a minimum and that a single, simple scene was
adequate and desirable.

Nothing could be more simple than the theme

and setting of *Lady Julia*, in which Strindberg
introduced startling experiments in form. Lady
Julia, the daughter of an ancient and noble house,
becomes the mistress of a valet, and kills herself
the following morning when realisation comes.
Strindberg has made of it a brilliant psychological
study, and technically the play is flawless. The
girl is neurotic, sensual, physically played out,
while the valet is virile and alive. He longs to
possess her, but she is an aristrocrat and it would
be sacrilege to make her his mistress. But then,
as she shows him favours, his vanity mounts higher
and higher until, when she has become his mistress, he tyrannises over her and reveals his mean
soul. She, the daughter of a dying family, had
thought to find renewal in his strength, but his
vulgarity and cruelty appal her. The only
solution is death.

In *Lady Julia*, as in *Creditors*, which succeeded
it, the action is continuous. Strindberg explains
that he has abolished the act division because he
believes that " our decreasing capacity for illusion
was possibly weakened by intervals in which the
spectator has time to reflect and thereby escape
from the suggestive influence of the author-
mesmerist." (He claimed later that the intervals
were introduced merely for the sake of the liquor
trade, and became in consequence a darling of the
temperance party in Sweden !)

With *Creditors*, Strindberg believed that he had
come nearer to the ideal form. " In a week." he

tells a friend, " I am sending you a new natural-istic drama better even than *Lady Julia*, with three characters, a table, and two chairs." Here, in *Creditors*, is the type of vampire woman, sucking at the life of her second husband after having tried to exhaust her first. But the super-man, in the person of the first husband, appears, and with diabolical cleverness shows the treacher-ous woman in her true character to the second husband. The latter dies of shock on discovering her infamy, and Tekla, the wife, bends over him with a cry. " Then," remarks the first husband in surprise, " you must have loved him too ! "

Tekla and Laura were the two characters of whom Strindberg was most proud in his natural-istic plays, and he believed that they had sug-gested *Hedda Gabler* to Ibsen. " Its parentage with Laura of *The Father* and Tekla of *Creditors* is undeniable," he writes. But Strindberg does not complain. He accepts it as reasonable that he, a genius, should be plundered ; and it flattered his vanity that " the Norwegian blue-stocking " should have to borrow from him !

Of the four plays, *Lady Julia* has remained the most popular. It was revived in London in 1933, but *The Father* is more familiar to English theatre-goers. *Lady Julia* had to wait nearly twenty years for its first production in Strindberg's native country, and then it was played before working-class audiences, who cheered " the fall of the aristocrat " and the triumph of the worker !

CHAPTER VI

(1889–1891)

Domestic tangles – goes to Denmark – establishes Scandinavian theatre– forbidden by the censor – anti-religious campaign – " a weapon of the rich " – return to Sweden – regarded as antichrist – theory of superman – correspondence with Nietzsche – fear of madness – divorced from Siri.

STRINDBERG's relations with his wife had become more and more unbearable. He regarded her as a demon, and imputed to her the most revolting crimes. She is the marauding Bertha of *Comrades*, for had not Siri tried to steal his fame ? In *The Father*, Strindberg is easily recognisable as the captain who is exposed to the wickedness of a woman without scruples, and he himself writes that it is part of his own life. In the play, Laura wishes to decide the education of the children, and at this time Strindberg and Siri were at logger-heads over the education of their three children. The wife throws doubts on the sanity of her husband in *The Father*, and Siri had in fact accused Strindberg of insanity a year before and applied to a doctor for confirmation. At the time, too, Strindberg was uncertain of the legitimacy of the children of his marriage with Siri, and he transferred those doubts to the captain.

Siri is clearly the neurotic, pleasure-loving, useless woman whom Strindberg draws in *Lady Julia*. She is the daughter of a decadent family and he himself has kinship with the valet in that he, as a man of plebeian blood, had hungered to win an aristocrat. " The son of the people has conquered the white skin," he had written of his marriage. " The plebeian has won the love of a woman of race, the swineherd has mixed his love with that of the princess." When, in *Creditors*, he makes Tekla a woman who sucks the brains of her second husband as she has done those of her first, he is making a charge that he often made against Siri. Tekla, too, is prepared to give herself to the first husband again, and Strindberg always suspected that Siri had spent afternoons of love with Baron Wrangel after her second marriage.

The trouble between Strindberg and Siri had become acute in the sixth or seventh year of marriage. Strindberg declares that they were never happy, but he himself has indicated the joy that he experienced with her as his wife in the early years. While in Stockholm at the time of his prosecution for *Married*, he had written her passionate love-letters, and in 1884 she had thanked him for " seven happy years." Helen Welinder, a friend who stayed with the Strindbergs in Switzerland in that year, writes of her experiences in *Memories of the Summer of 1884*. She did not form the opinion that they were as unhappy as Strindberg made out later, but it was clear to her that serious disagreement existed between husband and wife on certain points. Strindberg was violent at times, especially when the conversation turned to the failure to obtain production for his plays in Sweden. Then he would rave furiously against the " underground enemies " who were banded against him. It seemed to her that Strindberg was even then coming close to stepping over the " thin partition " that divides sanity from madness. Siri she found too much concerned with herself to give her husband that attention which might have relieved him of his fears : she wanted to build a life of her own apart from that of Strindberg.

After 1884, Strindberg left his wife on several occasions, and the project of complete separation appears to have been in his mind. Always, however, he returned to her after a short absence, eager for the Siri whom he despised but whom he needed. " I have to-day written two letters to my wife," he tells a friend. " In one of them I send her to the devil, in the other I ask her to return." In 1887 he went to Vienna, but no sooner was he parted from her than she received the most tender letters from him, and he hurried back to her side. Six months of happy love followed, and then, in November of the same year, Strindberg left for Denmark, where he remained till April, 1889.

He revived one of his old ideas – the establishment of an experimental theatre where Scandinavian dramatists of the new school could have their works performed and be independent of the commercial theatre. The Paris Théâtre Libre was chosen as the model, but the scheme was an abject failure. *The Father* and several of his other plays were, however, performed for the first time in Copenhagen, and Strindberg was in danger of becoming a social lion. A check saved him from that fate. The Danish censor refused to allow the production of *Lady Julia*, and Strindberg saw in the refusal the machinations of his enemies. Not only, he thought, were those enemies powerful in Sweden, where they prevented the production of his works, but they would not allow him even to live unmolested in another land. Strindberg dipped his pen in gall again and took up the lifelong struggle.

But the most important work of his first months in Denmark was the accusation hurled against the greatest enemy of all – his wife, Siri. He had for years harboured the suspicion that she had kept something hidden from him. Of her life in Finland before marriage with Baron Wrangel he could never discover anything, and so he suspected everything. He heard that rumours about her conduct were current in Stockholm, and he wrote to his brother asking him to find out what they were. " I must know or I shall go mad," he had written in 1887. He declares that he can withstand any blow, but that uncertainty will surely kill him. Strindberg himself paid a special visit in order to investigate.

He says that he had to interfere to prevent his wife from betraying him with a hall-porter on

one occasion and a local tradesman on another.
Nor, according to him, was Siri attracted only
by men. He charges her with Lesbianism, and
professes to have had definite proof; but while
he suspected that she had been the mistress of
other men, he could never be quite sure. And
he must know, for the legitimacy of the children
was at stake. " Only tell me," he pleads, " and
I shall forgive you." But Siri would never admit
the possibility that the children were not his, and,
like the captain in *The Father*, he tortured himself
in thinking that he was not the father.

Strindberg set traps for her – utilised the " new
psychology." He would introduce topics in conversation in the hope that she would make a slip ;
throw at his wife names of men with whom he
suspected her relations and watch whether she
gave any guilty signs ; he put books and articles
in her way which dealt with similar situations to
those he believed to exist with her, and studied
her face to see her reactions. He made life a hell
with his suspicions, both for himself and for her.
When she showed affection for him, Strindberg
could not accept it naturally. There must be a
reason, he would think ; and he decided that it
was because she had been unfaithful just before
and wanted to lull him into a feeling of false
security. Once he struck her in mad rage, and
she admitted infidelity to him on a single occasion. Repentant over the physical violence, he
forgave her and sought forgiveness for himself.

Then immediately he began again to search for proofs of further unfaithfulness.

Strindberg writes that in love he wanted to play the rôle of a child and find in the loved one a caressing mother ; he asked to be soothed and comforted, and instead Siri irritated and depressed him. He felt that his wife hated him because of his humble origin, and that she tried to disgrace him before their friends. Not only did she cajole him into agreement with proposals that he knew were wrong and unnecessary, but she wanted to triumph for the sake of triumphing. Strindberg claims that she neglected their children, yet at another time he wanted to get a divorce and pay Siri wages to act as governess to the children because she was necessary to them.

He spied through keyholes, hid himself in her room to listen to her conversation with the maid, opened her letters. He was convinced that she wanted to kill him, and believed that she had poisoned his food and set about rumours that he was mad. It indicates the state of Strindberg's mind at this time that he accused Ibsen of having written the *Wild Duck* against him ! And he assumes that the " celebrated Norwegian blue-stocking " was well bribed for writing the " scurrilous pamphlet," as he names one of Ibsen's most lovely pieces of work. Strindberg felt that the forces against him were too great and that his wife and her associates must inevitably over-come him in the end. He cries out that he is at the mercy of a vampire. He will struggle no longer to defend himself, but calmly await his fate.

The position of Siri was one of deep distress. She was not blameless in her treatment of Strindberg, but she was certainly not the unfeeling, treacherous fiend that he depicts. His attacks on women pained her ; the public naturally assumed that she must be in some part responsible for such views as he put forward with increasing violence. Even more painful to her than his attacks on women, however, were his criticisms of religious beliefs. He had in his youth been sincerely religious, and, although he had ceased to take any keen interest in religion after about his thirtieth year, he had still retained his faith. When, however, his anti-feminism grew to such alarming proportions, he examined everything to find points of attack so far as women were concerned. In the churches, women formed by far the majority of the worshippers, and Strindberg decided that it was because Christianity put them on a basis of equality with men. Religion therefore must be bad, and Strindberg began to attack it. Siri had always been devout, and she suffered deeply from her husband's outbursts against all that she held most sacred.

His anti-religious teachings lost him some of his Copenhagen friends, and as for the others, Strindberg came to believe that they had gone over to his enemies and were working for his undoing. He determined to escape from the

Fs

dangers which threatened him in Copenhagen,
and in 1889 he returned to Sweden. Strindberg
had known that feeling in Sweden had grown
against him on account of his anti-feminist and
anti-religious writings, but he had not anticipated
that he would be regarded with such absolute
hatred. He was considered a sort of antichrist,
and when collecting material for one of his books
was even refused permission to land on the west
coast, so great was the feeling against him. He
was more concerned at the check to his work
than displeased at the reception, for at this time
he was developing his theory of the superman and
it chimed in with his ideas that he should be
rejected by the vulgar mob. Since he had written
The Father, and first began to make the division
between the slave class and supermen like himself, the idea had assumed great proportions in
him and was to dominate his work for a period.

A powerful influence at this time was Edgar
Allan Poe. Strindberg had been introduced to
the American author's books, and found in them
much that coincided with his own theories. Poe
had died in 1849, the year of Strindberg's birth, and
Strindberg thought that this was significant. " Is
it possible," he writes in a letter, " that Poe's still
living flame could have been transmitted to me
across the years ? " Every book that he touched
immediately afterwards seemed to him to have
traces of Poe, and there is no limit to his admiration. In March, 1889, he refers to having

written " a brilliant **Edgar Poe.**" The play was
Simoon, and *Pariah,* also written at this time, is even
more clearly influenced by *Tales of Mystery and
Imagination. Pariah* was founded on a story by
Ola Hansson, a Swedish novelist, who had written
a book entitled *Pariahs* in which he shows the fate
of those who have transgressed the criminal laws.
Strindberg took the story and made of it an entirely different thing as a play – a duel between
two criminals ! Mr. X and Mr. Y are the characters. By masterly questioning, Mr. X ascer-
tains that Mr. Y is a thief, and he in turn con-
fesses that he committed a murder, though quite
unintentionally. Since he felt that he had no
right to bring disgrace to his parents and had his
work to perform in the world, Mr. X had not
given himself up to justice. Mr. Y, on hearing
this voluntary confession, tries to use the knowledge to force the murderer to steal valuables in
the room, but Mr. X is the superior mind and his
logic overcomes the thief, who creeps beaten from
the house.

In *Simoon,* Strindberg chooses a scene in Algeria.
A young lieutenant of Zouaves has become
separated from his regiment, and Biskra, an Arab
girl, determines to kill him by the power of suggestion as revenge for the dominion which the
French have acquired over the country. She
puts terrible thoughts into the wandering mind
of the lieutenant, who is suffering from fever in
the hot simoon wind. When he asks for water,

she makes him drink sand. She conjures up pictures of the unfaithfulness of his wife, of the death of his child, of the defeat of his regiment. When, overcome with shame and fear, he struggles up, she invites him to look at himself in a mirror and holds up a skull before his eyes. As he sinks back dead, a victim of the power of suggestion, her lover, Yusuf, comes in and hails her as fit to be the mother of Arab children.

Strindberg had sought more and more simplicity. He had cut down the number of characters, had set a stage that required practically no dressing, and had done away with the act division in an effort to focus attention on the psychological conflict. He wanted to refine the process still further and have a mere quarter of an hour of quick sustained action – " a battle of brains, a conflict of souls, a psychical struggle." *The Pariah* impresses by its brilliant dialogue, but *Simoon* goes too far and this barbaric little piece does not quite succeed. *Lady Julia* and *Creditors* marked the high-water mark of Strindberg's naturalism in the theatre, and most of the other naturalistic plays written after *Creditors* are disappointing. Mention should be made, however, of *The Stronger*, in which Strindberg carries the process of simplification still further. All the staging required is a table and two chairs, and the play is, in effect, a monologue. One woman, the wife, talks while the contribution of the second woman, the mistress of the other's husband, is limited to smiles

and gestures.   Yet the play is a supremely reveal-
ing psychological study of the wife, the mistress,
and the husband, and never fails to grip by its
subtle analysis when read or performed.   With
those one-act plays Strindberg said good-bye
to the theatre for several years.

In 1889, Strindberg had written a book of
stories, *Tschandala*, which caused Edmund Gosse to
refer to him as " the most remarkable creative
talent started by the philosophy of Nietzsche."
Strindberg, however, always declared that he
had worked out his idea of the master mind and
slave mind before he became acquainted with the
work of the German.   Nietzsche certainly affected
Strindberg strongly in *By the Open Sea*, written
a year later.   It is the story of a superman who as
a fishery expert is sent to an island to give the
benefit of his knowledge to the fishermen.   By
the use of his science he creates an illusion which
the fishermen think shows him to be possessed of
magic powers : and he so obviously despises the
humble folk, and makes himself so objectionable,
that they put every obstacle in the way of his
work.   The solitude, and the feeling that he is
wasted among such people, drive the hero of
By the Open Sea to madness and death.   Strindberg
claimed that he, like Axel Borg in *By the Open Sea*,
had been constantly impeded by the stupidity of the
slave class. He declared himself to be above ordinary moral laws, which applied only to common
people, and demanded that to him as a superman

the world should supply according to his needs.

A short correspondence took place between Strindberg and Nietzsche at the end of 1888. Georg Brandes had drawn Nietzsche's attention to the work of Strindberg and advised him to read the Swede's books, which reflected something of Nietzsche's ideas, especially in regard to women. Nietzsche, who had just finished *Ecce Homo* and was then living in Italy, opened the correspondence with a letter to Strindberg in which he explained that the message he wished to give to the world required an audience larger than Germany alone could provide. Strindberg read *Thus Spake Zarathustra*, and congratulated Nietzsche on writing the deepest book possessed by mankind. As for the people with whom Strindberg was living, Nietzsche could judge their intelligence by the fact that they wanted to confine him in an asylum on account of *The Father*.

Nietzsche found in *The Father* a work in which his own conception of love – " with war as its means and the deathly hate of the sexes as its fundamental law " – was splendidly expressed, and asked Strindberg to translate *Ecce Homo* into French and English. Strindberg refused to undertake a French translation without adequate payment, and as for England, he advised Nietzsche to ignore it, since England was " a puritan land delivered into the hands of women – which is the same thing as having fallen into a state of absolute decadence. English morality –

you know what that is, my dear sir ! " He also complained that an old lady fell dead during the performance of *The Father*, another woman fainted, and "when the strait-jacket was produced on the stage, three-quarters of the audience rose like one man and ran from the theatre bellowing like bulls."

Strindberg had forwarded a book to Nietzsche, and received the following letter :

" You will have an answer to your story in due course – it sounds like a rifle-shot. I have commanded a royal holiday at Rome – I wish to order a fusillade.

" Until we meet again ! For we shall meet again.

" A single condition : *divorçons*.

" NIETZSCHE CÆSAR."

The letter puzzled Strindberg, but he replied in a mixture of Greek and Latin :

" Not without perturbation did I receive your letter, and I thank you for it.

" Adieu, and keep in kind remembrance,

" YOUR STRINDBERG.

" (The best, the highest God.) "

A single line was returned :

" Herr Strindberg : Eheu ! No more ! *Divorçons*.

" THE CRUCIFIED ONE."

Nietzsche was removed to an asylum shortly

afterwards, and remained there until his death ten years later. Strindberg had not realised that he was communicating with a madman, and feared that he would be regarded as insane for his part in the correspondence. Maupassant was removed to an asylum in the same year, and Strindberg began to have a suspicion that the world was locking up all the great men and that he would be the next to go into an asylum. He had applied to an asylum for a certificate of sanity, but was told that he must remain under observation for several weeks. Strindberg refused to agree to that course. He felt that once he entered the asylum, his wife would ensure that he never got out.

In the meantime, he had other worries. He was being pressed for money on every side, was drinking heavily, and did not seem to have a friend left. It was at this time (1891) that proceedings for divorce between Siri and Strindberg were started. His wife turned up before a tribunal in a state of intoxication, but, although she was severely reprimanded, the court decided that she should have the custody of the three children of the marriage. Strindberg was deeply wounded that the children had been taken away from him, and writes to a friend at this time of his fear that they would be brought up to "forget and hate me."

Even at the time of the divorce, he still yearned for the woman whom he had accused of the most frightful crimes. "My God," he writes, "how tenacious is love ! "

CHAPTER VII

(1891–1894)

AFTER the divorce, Strindberg fled from society and hid himself on an island near Stockholm. He wrote very little, for it seemed to him useless to engage in literary work. Dramas that he knew to be among his best could not obtain production in Sweden : his books were refused by Swedish publishers, who would not risk the consequences of publishing his work. Since writing had failed him, he took up his brushes again and painted with passionate energy. The sea had always had a fascination for him and most of his paintings were sea studies. His technical knowledge was not great, but he painted with a keen feeling, and the pictures created a sensation. But they did not bring profit to him, and the exhibition that he held in Stockholm was a financial failure.

He was deeply in debt ; requests for money for the support of his children could not be met, and he had to beg for food. Small sums came to him from time to time, but most of it went in drink. That was his only relief. His letters were full of complaints and heart-rending appeals for assistance. The writing is the writing of a man who cannot hold his pen steady. In January, 1892, he says that he has to pawn his clothes, and nearly all his letters at this time end, " if I live and I preserve my reason." He suffered from agoraphobia, and the persecution mania had begun to seize him yet more strongly. It must be persecution, he thought, when a man who had written " the best modern drama, and had invented a new form of play with a new plot," could not earn enough to support himself and his children. The cares with which he was surrounded made him incapable of work. He wondered again if he were going mad, and to reassure himself adds to a letter, " Yet I am not a decadent type, for I represent the height gained by the family of Strindberg."

His appeals brought little financial assistance, for Strindberg had quarrelled with most of his friends. Relations of any kind seemed to him to interfere with his development ; he felt that friendship limited him, and then he was brutal in breaking the connection. The case of Björnson, the Norwegian dramatist, also a rebel, though a more pleasant one than Strindberg, may be mentioned. Björnson had a sincere admiration for Strindberg's work and offered to help the young author. As a man of established reputation he was in a position to render valuable service during Strindberg's early years of striving, and Strindberg was flattered by the commendation of such a man. But when Björnson offered some sound criticism, Strindberg took it amiss ; he resented criticism of any kind, and wrote in reply : " Your Majesty, I have received your imperial command and have the honour to ignore it altogether." So it was with all Strindberg's friendships. In time – usually a short time – he found them cramping and broke them as offensively as possible.

Ola Hansson, the Swedish novelist, and his wife, Laura Marholm, heard of Strindberg's plight, and invited him to come to Berlin, where they were then living ; but Strindberg had no money for the journey and could not leave until certain pressing debts were paid. Since his appeals had become more and more pitiful, they decided to ask the public for assistance, and Hansson wrote an article describing Strindberg's position and offered to start a fund. The article was published in the German *Zukunft* and met with a generous enough response. The money was sent to Strindberg and he gladly left Stockholm. Strindberg is described as looking much older than his age on his arrival in Berlin ; the tawny hair had turned grey suddenly, and he talked in a weak and quavery voice, like an old man. He could not bear to meet a direct glance, and was suspicious of all the world.

He arrived in a fury. How dare they, he asked, write a begging article about him ? Strindberg accused Hansson and his wife of trying to ruin his reputation ;   Laura Marholm he anathematised as a creature of the feminists who wanted to represent him in the worst possible light before the public. The Hanssons realised that they were dealing with a sick man, and helped Strindberg in every way.

Under their care he grew stronger, and the new friends he made helped him to forget his grievances against the world. In a little café in the Unter den Linden, christened by Strindberg "Zum schwarzen Ferkel" ("The Black Pig"), he formed a group of young writers and artists over whom he held undisputed sway. One of them was Stanilaus Prsybyszevski, a Polish novelist, who called the Swede "master" and thought no sacrifice too great for his beloved Strindberg. A few years later, Strindberg was to believe that Prsybyszevski was hounding him to death. Another member of the group was Adolf Paul, who became a very close friend but later quarrelled with Strindberg. Paul wrote a book about the friendship, *Strindberg-Erinnerungen und Briefe*, which is a rancorous piece of work. But the quarrels were still in the future, and for the present Strindberg was happy enough, singing songs of his own composition to the guitar, lording it over the youthful aspirants and carousing nightly. One other member of the group must be mentioned – Dagny Juel, the woman whom Strindberg calls Aspasia in his later books and who was his mistress at this period.

Strindberg began to feel secure again, and he

returned to writing. Four one-act plays, *Facing Death*, *The First Warning*, *Debit and Credit*, and *Mother Love*, were written in 1893, but none of them is of much importance. They mark the end of Strindberg's naturalistic period, with the exception of two plays which appeared some years later, *Playing with Fire* and *The Bond*. The latter play is the story of his divorce from Siri, and is a moving piece of work which reveals Strindberg's concern for the children of parents who dissolve the marriage tie. Of the last group of naturalistic plays, it is by far the most effective.

Strindberg had lived a Bohemian life in Berlin, but suddenly he changed, and, to the surprise of his café friends, became " respectable " and blossomed out as a man of fashion. Everyone who knew the misery of his first marriage, and of his relief at putting the cares of family life behind him, were astonished when he announced his engagement to Frida Uhl. But Strindberg explains that " he would – he must – have a woman to worship," and his choice for this rôle was a young Austrian, again the daughter of an aristocratic family. Frida's father was attached to the Austrian Court and opposed the marriage, calling Strindberg a mad and ungodly writer and refusing to meet " the nihilist." Frida was unmoved by the protests of her parents and grandparents, and the marriage took place in April, 1893.

Strindberg and Frida went to England, primarily as a honeymoon trip, but also with the view

of securing production for some of his plays.
First they lived in Gravesend and then came to
London. England impressed Strindberg favourably at the beginning of the stay. " England is
fine," he writes. " The ale is strong, the gin
weak," but he could not eat the food. The flowers
pleased him, and he calls England a " southern
land," but he was appalled by the poverty and
wretchedness, which were worse than he had seen
in any of the ten capitals he knew. London to
him was a place of " perfect tropical heat. . . .
From morning till evening one feels only half
alive." It was in London that he had the first
of the hallucinations which were to make his life
a misery in the next few years. While crossing
Waterloo Bridge, the beggars seemed to assume
terrific proportions and descend upon him *en
masse*. Another danger was the police. Frida
kissed him in the street, and Strindberg was
afraid of being arrested for such a display of
feeling in the unemotional land that is England !

After two months in England, Strindberg went
to Hamburg but left his wife in London. He told
Paul, whom he met in Hamburg, that he had fled
from the " dangers of London," but the real
reason for his departure was dissatisfaction with
Frida. She was an author and translator, and
they found themselves unable to write in each
other's company.   " They   neutralised   each
other," says Strindberg in the story which describes the marriage and which is written in the

third person. " The need to be near each other
was so great that one could not leave the room
without the other following. They tried to shut
themselves in their rooms in order to work, but
after a short time one would knock at the other's
door. . . . They were apparently so harmonious
in all questions and predilections, and knew each
other's opinions so well, that there was no further
need to exchange thoughts. . . . Each had lost
individuality and they were one. But the
memory of independence and one's own personality was still present, and a war of liberation
was impending. The sense of personal self-
preservation awoke, and, when each wished to
resume their own share, there was a strife about
the pieces."

In a quarrel between them, she had thrown
doubts on the value of his work and said that she
would translate more important authors than
him. That his own wife should speak of his books
disrespectfully was to Strindberg the last indignity.
" He felt the bond between them snap. She hated
and despised his work . . . she was the enemy.
And in dealing with an enemy there are only two
methods – either to kill him, or not to fight him
but to flee." Strindberg fled.

When he was in Hamburg, Strindberg yearned
for his wife again. She wrote often, but the correspondence was unsatisfactory. In one of her
letters she dwelt on her inextinguishable love,
and compared them to Hero and Leander,

separated by the English Channel. In the next, she spoke of raising capital to open a theatre in London (but could not find enough money for her fare to Hamburg !), and followed it by complaining that he had left his sick wife in a foreign land. A fourth letter said that she was in a convent, and in that letter " she also denounced the wickedness of the world and the hell of marriage. It was impossible to give reasonable answers to those letters, for they poured on him like hail and crossed his own. If he wrote a gentle reply, he received a scolding letter in answer to a previous sharp one of his, and vice versa. Their misunderstandings arrived at such a pitch that they bordered on lunacy, and when he ceased to write she began to send telegrams."

That is Strindberg's story. Adolf Paul says that, in Hamburg, Strindberg was a prey to terrors and talked about the menace of " brigands." So alarming did his condition appear that Paul wrote to Frida asking her to come to her husband, but she replied that she could not leave London (the negotiations regarding the production of Strindberg's plays in London were, however, unsuccessful in the end). Strindberg went about Hamburg like a madman, but was relieved from his perplexities by an invitation to stay with Frida's father at Mondsee, near Salzburg, where his wife would join him. His mother-in-law and father-in-law, who did not appear to agree on anything else, both warned him that

Frida was " difficult." Strindberg's views on women were especially approved by his father-in-law, who remarked, " You have written all that I wished to write."

Meanwhile, the arrival of Frida at Mondsee was expected, but she did not appear. Strindberg went to Berlin to await her, and lived in a little village outside the capital. When he returned in the evening, he saw people at the windows of the houses regarding him in a furtive manner with wild, distracted looks, and immediately afterwards shyly hiding themselves behind the curtains. This could have only one interpretation to Strindberg – the people thought him mad ! Later he discovered that the village was one in which harmless lunatics were boarded out. He had another experience in this village. To while away the time, he decided to ascertain whether apples were sensitive to poison, and went out one day with a morphia syringe. He found an apple-tree which appeared suitable for the experiment, and made an insertion with the syringe. He had pressed too hard, and the apple fell, while at the same time he saw an angry man, followed by his wife and child, running towards him with uplifted stick and shouting, " There ! I have him at last."

He " was mistaken for an apple-stealer for whom they had been watching," he writes. " Like one condemned to death," he waited for the man to arrive. " He was firmly resolved to

Gs

die like a warrior, and did not trouble to devise useless explanations, but only thought, ' This is the most devilish experience I have had in my whole terrible life.' " But the owner of the apples took no action. Worse than any action that he might have taken was that he regarded Strindberg as a lunatic from the village !

Frida joined her husband in Berlin and they swore never to leave each other again, " not even for half a day." But discord soon arose between them, though each appears to have tried hard to be forbearing towards the other. Strindberg had little respect for his wife's talents as a writer and thought that she exaggerated the importance of her work. When she became pregnant, Frida accused him of having wanted a child only to " spoil her career " and Strindberg had no patience with her complaints. She left for her native country, but after a time she invited her husband to join her at the home of her grandparents on the Danube. They were happy together and once more swore eternal fidelity, but, though Strindberg was on the best of terms with Frida, he soon quarrelled with her grandfather. Strindberg was working at this time on *Antibarbarus*, in which he put forward some startling scientific theories, and, knowing the opinion that others would hold of them, he tried to keep the work secret. The grandfather was persistent, and, on learning of the nature of the theories, laughed them to scorn. Frida appealed to her husband to control himself, but the enmity between him and the old man flared out at intervals. It was in connection with proceedings that had been taken in Berlin over *The Confession of a Fool* that the final break came. The book had been suppressed – the translation gave a wrong impression of the work – and Strindberg was summoned to court. He refused to appear, on the ground that as a Swede he was not answerable to a foreign court, but the grandfather took a different view, and Strindberg, who was never accommodating, did not explain his attitude. As a result of the quarrel, Frida and he were told to clear out, but a small cottage belonging to the family was given to them.

"In this cottage," writes Strindberg, " began the two happiest months in the life of this happy pair." But after the two months were over, the troubles started all over again between them. The child – the only child of the marriage with Frida – was born, and " cried all day." The peasants pointed out that this was because the baby was not baptised, and the grandmother pressed Strindberg to have it baptised as a Catholic. Strindberg, a thorough-going atheist, replied by letter, " We Protestants are very tolerant in our belief, but if it is made a financial matter, we can be as fanatical as some Catholics." The answer was an order to vacate the cottage – and Strindberg did not possess a penny for travelling expenses. He returned, " To be a martyr for a faith which one does not possess is somewhat fantastic," but warned his grandparents that as a husband he had rights which he might use later if they were unreasonable over the baptism. The child was baptised in Strindberg's absence, and its crying became normal. Strindberg was assured that the child had been baptised as a Protestant – but a Catholic had performed the ceremony !

Strindberg felt that he had been over-reached, and he decided that he would no longer remain in the humiliating position of having to depend on his wife's relatives for a home. His plays were being performed in Paris, and he made up his mind to go there – as soon as he could get money. Frida implored him to take her, but he refused to allow her to leave the child. She believed that he was trying to desert her, and accused him of having no interest in the child. Strindberg says that he feared to become too much attached to the baby, for " he felt that a separation from the mother was in the air, and to be tied to her by means of the child he felt to be a fetter."

The money for his journey did not come, and Strindberg was treated as a worthless and superfluous member of the household. Frida had turned against him and joined with her relatives in the petty persecution. When he was ill, they would not send for a doctor. Never, he told Frida, had he seen such intense malice in anyone. " And he wept, perhaps for the first time for

twenty years," Strindberg writes of himself as
the hero of his story. " It seemed monstrous that
he, a distinguished man in his own line, should,
through no fault of his own, lead such a wretched
life that even the maidservant pitied him. Since
he had entered his relatives' house, his behaviour
had been unimpeachable. He did not even drink,
if only for the reason that there was nothing to
drink."

When the money for the journey arrived,
Strindberg gave way to his wife's tearful appeal
and agreed to take her with him to Paris, leaving
the child in the care of her parents, but he felt
that a final separation was near. " My marriage
will not last, that's sure," he writes to a friend.
It was in August 1894 that Strindberg and Frida
arrived in Paris. In less than three months the
parting took place.

Returning from the station after saying good-
bye to Frida, he writes, " I place myself at the
table where I used to sit with my wife, my beautiful jailkeeper, who watched my soul day and
night, guessed my secret thoughts, marked out the
course of my ideas, and was jealous of my investi-
gations into the unknown."

Tragedy had never been far from Strindberg,
but now came the period of deepest darkness in
his burdened life.

CHAPTER VIII

(1894–1898)

In Paris, Strindberg had won a great victory.
The dream of every Scandinavian dramatist was
to obtain production in the French capital, and
it had been Strindberg's ambition for years.
Now it was achieved – and before Ibsen, who was
still unknown in the Paris theatres, though twenty-
one years the senior of Strindberg. Apart from
the fact that he had succeeded where Ibsen had
failed, however, Strindberg had no pleasure in his
triumph. His plays had ceased to interest him
and he did not go near the theatres where they
were performed.

Managers sought his work ; journalists wished
to interview him ; photographers asked for
appointments ; and he was the literary man of
the day – at one time six of his plays were running
simultaneously in Paris. He had been offered the
Legion of Honour by the French Government on
the publication of his monograph, *Relations
between France and Sweden*, but Strindberg politely
refused, giving as his excuse that he " never wore
a frock-coat." The publisher of the work was,

however, a Swede, and bureaucracy was satisfied by decorating the publisher in place of the author.

An invitation came to him to go to Berlin, where, on his previous visit, he had been fêted as the leader of the new theatre and his arrival heralded in verse – "An Immortal – To Germany's Guest." But Strindberg had no desire to enjoy literary fame in Paris or Berlin. His ambition was to prove the truth of the startling theories he had enunciated in *Antibarbarus*. The chemical theories of the book had been treated with scorn as the fancies of an untrained amateur, "the work of a charlatan or madman," and he could not rest until the critics retracted. Only science had significance to him now.

He took a little room in the Latin Quarter and applied himself to the proof of his theories. Here were secrets which had defied mankind through the ages, and it was left to him to solve them and so benefit the world. It seemed a task worthy of the superman of Nietzsche, and would make his name live for ever. Strindberg was in abject poverty ; he rarely stirred out of doors, refused the invitations which rolled in, and spent his days over the totally inadequate chemical apparatus that he had constructed. While studying medicine with Dr. Lamm, he had taken a course at the Technological Institute in Stockholm, but his knowledge of chemistry was not extensive.

The renunciation of the long coveted triumph in the Paris theatres appealed to the dramatic in

Strindberg ; but his preoccupation with science was no mere pose. He would have sacrificed anything for the sake of his chemical researches at this time. Indeed, he felt that he had sacrificed Frida on the altar of science. In her letters, she appealed to him to surrender his mad experiments and enjoy the fame earned by years of striving, and Strindberg decided that it must be his wife or his chemistry. There was no hesitation in his own mind as to which was the more important. He pretended that he had taken a mistress, and wrote to her an " unpardonable letter " in which he announced the wholly fictitious love-affair. She answered with a demand for separation. Strindberg had expected nothing else, but he was nevertheless shocked to receive her reply. He tried to find his consolation in science – " positive science, which alone is of value " – but sometimes he wept over the situation into which " his duty " had brought him. " I see myself so abominably treated by mankind that I weep over myself as if it were another man who suffered, in all innocence, the tortures of hell," he writes. " But the substance of my brain is not corrupted ; it works so well, so well."

Later he writes, " I am surrounded by silence and loneliness. . . . My hands are black and bleeding – black as misery, bleeding as my heart." His hands had been neglected and were actually " black and bleeding." The news of his position reached the Scandinavian colony in

Paris, and a collection was made to pay his hotel
bill so that he could be removed to hospital for the
treatment that was so urgently needed. One of
the doctors supported his chemical theories, and
Strindberg, on his discharge from hospital, was
encouraged to continue his experiments. First he
meant to demonstrate that sulphur contained
carbon and he was of opinion that he had succeeded. The result of his experiments was
published in French newspapers, and he was
delighted at the reception his work received.
There were many critics, but he had also a strong
body of adherents, some of whom were distinguished men. After this preliminary success,
Strindberg went further and believed that he had
found the philosopher's stone and could make
gold. Years later he was convinced that the
American Government had stolen his secret and
that gold was being made in Washington according to his formula !

The gold-making experiments were scorned,
and Strindberg found that his critics were growing
in number. Not only had he active opponents
here on earth, however, but he believed that there
were " invisible powers " who sought to prevent
him from triumphing. He refers to the " unknown powers which have persecuted me for
years and frustrate my endeavours " ; but he
discovered that there were also benignant powers
who wished to help him, though they imposed
strict discipline in return. When he errs, he is

punished with punctuality and exactness, but when he has proved himself humble, then the good powers come to his aid at times of deepest depression. The beneficent powers were kind to him in the summer and autumn, and he counted the period as " on the whole among the happiest stages of my eventful life." Money flowed in from admirers, and he could buy books and scientific instruments, while other friends " bring me food as the ravens did to Elijah."

He read religious works of all kinds, and believed that a " kind of religion was forming," although he could not formulate it distinctly. Sar Péladan impressed him greatly ; he found comfort in *The Imitation of Christ* ; at other times he delved into standard works on mysticism and occultism. Buddhism drew him powerfully. " A Buddhist book has a stronger influence on me than all other sacred books," he writes, " because it ranks positive suffering above mere abstinence." There were moods of deepest pessimism when he cried, " Let us therefore suffer without hoping for any real joy in life – for, my brothers, we are in hell." Then he would be uplifted by the inter-vention of the beneficent powers. They ruled the smallest details of his life, even telling him when he might drink coffee and when such an indul-gence was forbidden !

An overwhelming desire for his wife seized him at times, and he determined to bring about a reconciliation by means of witchcraft. " I

believed myself in possession of unlimited strength,
and pride inspired me with the wild idea of seeing
whether I could perform a miracle." The miracle
he sought to accomplish was to bring about the
illness of the only child of his second marriage by
telepathic influence. Strindberg had always
been able to exert strong telepathic powers, and
he grew to believe that there was no limit to his
ability to wound at a distance by " willing " harm
to absent persons. He offered to remove any of
Brandes's enemies by sticking pins in their photo-
graphs and wishing them evil ! It was a terrible
power, says Strindberg, but he is complacent
enough about it. On the day after the publication of an article in which he criticised the current
astronomical theories, one famous astronomer
died, and shortly afterwards the death of a
second occurred. Strindberg had no doubt
of the connection between his article and their
demise !

The miracle went astray on this occasion.
Strindberg had wished to cause his child to be ill
enough only to alarm Frida. Then, thought
Strindberg, he would be hurriedly summoned to
the sick child whose illness he had brought about,
and what moment could be more favourable for
reconciliation with the anxious mother than that
of a common misfortune ? He set to work " with
the picture of my dear little daughter." Alas for
witchcraft ! The daughters of his first marriage
fell ill and Frida's child escaped scatheless.

Strindberg was sure that he was responsible for the illness of the children of his first marriage, and that his attempt to intervene in such a way drew upon him the " mercilessness of the unknown powers." " The hand of the invisible is lifted," he writes, " and the blows fall heavily." Everything began to go wrong. The printing of a book on which he had set his heart, and which he was publishing at his own expense, cost double what was agreed upon, and he had to pawn his clothes and instruments to pay the bill. When *Sylva Sylvarum* was printed, however, he felt " uplifted at having done something original, great, and beautiful for the first time in my life." But the powers did not content themselves with causing financial stringency. They brought about the interruption of his work in various ways, and Strindberg arrived " at an ever clearer conviction that the Eternal has handed me over to Satan to be tried."

He thought that the anti-feminists were pursuing him, and when a doctor advised him to take up hard physical exercise such as wood-chopping to get rid of his fears, Strindberg wanted to know whether wood-chopping was of any use against women ! His most persistent enemy, however, was, in Strindberg's opinion, Prsybyszevski (whom he calls Popoffsky). Prsybyszevski had married Dagny Juel, who had been Strindberg's mistress, and Strindberg was convinced that Prsybyszevski wanted to kill him in revenge. Warnings came

from all sides. In the park he found two twigs
which formed the Greek letters " p " and " y "
– the first and last letters of Popoffsky. He visited
a friend of Popoffsky, but a huge dog lying in the
courtyard was a signal that danger lurked in the
house ; a further visit was stopped by the sight
of a child playing with a card which Strindberg
recognised just in time as an unlucky one !

People hammered nails in the room above and
kept him from concentrating. A family took up
quarters in the same house and " for a day and
night crying babies afford me much pleasure and
remind me of the good old times when I was
between thirty and forty and life was pleasant."
He thought his food was poisoned ; another time
he suspected that gas was being discharged
through a pipe into his room. The occupant of
the room next door appeared to do everything
that Strindberg did, and Strindberg feared him as
an enemy who had come to take his life. He felt
an electric current passing between the two rooms
and ran out in terror. In the room that he found
in another house there was a temporary lull, but
the horrors and hallucinations soon recommenced.
He heard preparations being made in the room
above his and prepared for his last day, burning
all his papers, writing letters of farewell, and
dressing himself in his best clothes. At two o'clock
in the morning – the attacks on his life always
came at exactly this hour – the electric current
struck him and he was pressed to the ground.

Strindberg fled from the room and spent the rest of the night in the garden.

On the following day he went to friends in Dieppe. " Where have you come from ? " they asked at the sight of his haggard face and his wild, staring eyes. " From the dead," Strindberg replied. Their care could not remove his fears. In the middle of the night, the electric current again struck him at the fatal hour and Strindberg rushed to another room prepared for him to meet just such an emergency. In the morning he set out for Sweden, and lived for a time with a friend, Dr. Eliasson, in Ystad. Dr. Eliasson undertook to treat him, and Strindberg agreed to submit to treatment for the insanity which had been growing on him for years. To some extent it was due to his drinking excesses ; he had taken absinthe in large quantities for a very long time.

Strindberg was obedient enough at first, but then his suspicions broke out again. How could he be mad when his writings were published in the foremost papers in Europe throughout the whole of the period ? The doctor tried patiently to explain the position, but Strindberg was not satisfied. He decided that Dr. Eliasson wanted to steal the secret of how to make gold, and regarded him as an enemy thereafter.

An improvement took place in his condition, but he was still a long way from complete recovery when he insisted on leaving Dr. Eliasson's house and going to Frida's mother in September, 1896.

He had thought her a strange woman at the first
meeting, and a better acquaintance only con-
firmed that opinion. She had, however, much to
do with his return to sanity.

While in Paris, Strindberg had been drawn to
Swedenborg's works by the reading of Balzac's
Seraphita, but had not made a detailed study of
Swedenborgianism. His mother-in-law, well
versed in the religion, now introduced him to
further works, and Strindberg was tremendously
impressed and comforted. The Swedenborgian
doctrine taught him that his sufferings were for
his past misdeeds, and that the purgatory through
which he was passing represented merely a necessary stage in the journey towards a higher life.
Strindberg discovered that the trials of Swedenborg, a Swede like himself, were exactly those that
he had to endure, and he accepted an explanation which, by showing that the tortures had a
purpose, liberated him from the fear of them to a
great extent. Swedenborg, Strindberg wrote,
" has frightened me back to God " and " shown
me the only path to salvation : to seek out
the demons from their dens within myself and
to kill them – by repentance." He dedicated
one of his books " To Emanuel Swedenborg,
Teacher and Leader, This book is dedicated by
his disciple."

Though Strindberg never wholly accepted the
Swedenborgian doctrine, it had a calming effect
on him, and the presence of the little daughter of

his second marriage also helped him to recover
his sanity ; but he was not yet at the end of his
dolorous way.   The persecution mania returned,
the electric girdle sometimes came to seize him,
and at intervals he found the hand of Popoffsky
threatening him with death once more.   Strange
things happened in the house, and his mother-in-
law, who had hoped to complete his cure through
the Swedenborgian doctrines, found the task too
much for her.   Strindberg's " demons " interfered in everything and made life in the house a
succession of awful terrors.   " Depart, my son,"
she said at last, " for I am sick of this odour
of hell."

Strindberg went to Lund, a small University
town in Sweden, where he lived for several months
and steadily regained his mental powers.   The
desire to write returned to him, and he wrote the
story of his sufferings in *Inferno*, which owes much
to Poe in conception.   No more remarkable
analysis of the mental derangement of a man of
great intellectual power has ever been published.
It is more than a study in mental pathology : in
Inferno Strindberg bares his soul, and the book is
an extraordinarily vivid description of the working of the mind of a genius hovering on the border-
line of madness and at times crossing the boundary
into insanity, but never incapable of acute observation and almost brutal self-revelation.

The book, and the sequel, *Legends*, ought, in
Strindberg's opinion, to warn the world.   " Such

then is my life," he ends *Inferno*, " an example to serve for the betterment of others, a proverb to set forth the nothingness of fame and celebrity ; a proverb to show the younger generation how they should not live. Yes, I am a proverb ; I, who regarded myself as a prophet, am revealed as a braggart. Now, the eternal has led this false prophet to seek empty words, and the false prophet feels irresponsible since he has only played the rôle assigned to him."

But Strindberg did not always feel irresponsible for what he had taught in the first forty years of his life. He underwent agonies of repentance in Lund, and declares : " I find my past life abominable and am disgusted at my own personality "; he did not seek to shirk the responsibility, but felt that he must do penance for his crimes. The students came to him as the most distinguished author of their country, and he found their homage comforting. Not only did students sit at his feet, but he had also the society and admiration of those who, like himself, were " damned souls in hell," punished " ceaselessly and remorselessly " though less able to bear the torments. One gathers the impression from *Legends* that Lund was peopled with " damned souls " who lived the most painful and complicated lives. But many of the stories Strindberg tells were of his own imagining.

To Strindberg, however, everything in *Legends* was terribly real. Although he had managed to

Hs

free himself from some of the terrors that had
previously assailed him, he still suffered from the
powers who had been deputed to punish him for
his past mistakes. The electric girdle continued
to encircle him, and he had constriction of the
chest, difficulty of breathing, symptoms of suffoca-
tion, terrible attacks of fear. In the middle of the
night he would be thrown to the floor and feel
himself assailed by devils. Strindberg condemned all his past writings, and hoped that the
confession of his past mistakes would mitigate his
offences ; but his anti-feminism still possessed
him and he withdrew nothing that he had written
against women. In his diary for 1897 he quotes
with approval the words of St. Chrysostom :
" What is woman ? The enemy of friendship,
the punishment that cannot be escaped, the
necessary evil, the natural temptation, the longed-
for misery, the fountain of tears which is never
dry, the worst masterpiece of creation in white and
dazzling array."

Life in Lund seemed to him confining, and
Strindberg pined for the activity of Paris. Before
he could make the move, however, he had to
receive the permission of the powers, but there
were so many contrary signs that Strindberg was
driven to the conclusion that the powers " are
not agreed among themselves and that I am the
object of protracted discussion. One urges me
on, another holds me back." On the 24th of
August, 1897, he writes, " I get out of bed, pull

up the window-blind, and see a crow standing on
the chimney of a very high house. It stands like
a cock on the tower of Notre-Dame and looks as
though it were about to fly towards the south."
The bird comes first towards Strindberg and then
wings its way southwards. What clearer message
could the powers send? Strindberg packed up
and departed for Paris.

In Paris, Strindberg set himself to write, but the
powers had not finished with him and interfered
with his work. Strindberg determined that there
was nothing left for him but a monastery, and
made enquiries about being received into a
Catholic institution in Belgium. He is preparing
to bury himself there when he reads in a newspaper that the abbot of the monastery has been
deposed for immorality. To Strindberg this is
a clear sign that he is not meant to adopt the
monastic life. " A Trappist may confess to the
priests," he writes, " but for my part it is enough
that my sin be publicly acknowledged."

Strindberg passed through many stages in his
religious crisis. He emerged from it with his
mind full of strange and opposing philosophies,
with a firm belief that our hell is here on earth
and that everything has significance, and that
from him as the most miserable of sinners a great
penance was required. No Church could ever
claim him as a member, though he seriously
considered Roman Catholicism ; and he would
have been an embarrassing adherent to any

sect. But after his madness he returned to the
certainty that there was a God, and his seeking was
the seeking of a believer. Till the end of his
life his religious beliefs took varied forms, but
Strindberg never again lost the simple, childlike
faith in a deity strong to punish and quick to
reward.

CHAPTER IX

(1898–1902)

STRINDBERG had been looked upon as a man who
was finished so far as literary production was concerned, but now he amazed everyone by the
quantity of the work which he produced as well
as by its quality. While " the powers " still in-
tervened in the choice of subjects, they allowed
him a wide choice, and he poured out plays,
stories, and articles with amazing speed. Mysticism and symbolism now dominated his work,
though at times he reverted to the naturalism of
ten years ago.

His first great work was *To Damascus*, one of the
strangest plays that has ever been given to the
world. It is a mixture of naturalism and super-
naturalism, introducing new and startling ideas in
dramatic technique and forming a remarkable
confession. Strindberg is relentless towards himself in *To Damascus*, and tells there the story of his
deepest distress. It is the tale of the powers of
good and evil fighting in the soul of Strindberg,
and reveals how he has battled with the powers of
darkness as well as denied the powers of light.

The drama suggests the miracle play. There is

the Stranger (Strindberg), the Lady (Frida Uhl),
the Beggar, the Doctor, the Old Man, the Mother,
the Confessor, the Tempter, etc.   It starts with the
meeting between the Stranger and the Lady.   He
says that he has waited forty years for something
which he believes is called happiness, but which
may be only the end of misery.   The Lady asks
whether he has never had any joy in life, and the
Stranger replies that when he seemed to find joy
it turned out to be poisoned on every occasion.
He admits that he has had all that he demanded
from life, but that it proved to be quite worthless.
He was born and brought up in hatred, and all his
life he has been hated because he would not submit to be duped.   The world has cast him out
because he could not bear to see men suffer ; he
had tried to help men and women towards freedom and a fuller life, and worst of all in the eyes of
the world was that he had said to the children,
" Disobey your parents when they are unjust."
He does not wish the Lady happiness, because
" that does not exist."

The Stranger seeks the Lady's company for his
journey, and points to his misery and loneliness
as a reason why she should accompany him.   She
must, however, go back to her husband, the Werewolf.   When she has gone, the Beggar appears
and talks Latin ; the Stranger turns from him in
disgust, but when the Lady comes back she
explains that when the Stranger is drunk he
resembles the Beggar.   She has returned to ask

the Stranger to release her from the Werewolf;
when the Stranger sees the Werewolf, he recognises him as one to whom he had done an injury
as a schoolboy. A lunatic, Cæsar, a name by
which Strindberg had been known, appears, and
the Stranger and the Lady flee in terror from him.

Their wanderings begin, and they arrive at a
hotel penniless and regarded as " not respectable."
Both have been in the same hotel room before,
but in different circumstances, and Strindberg
brings in the theme of eternal repetition, of re-
living the past. They feel that " the powers "
are dogging them, and go to a cottage in the
mountain. It is spring, and in peacefulness they
know a few days of keenest happiness. The
Stranger wants to die, but the Lady feels that she
must " suffer further." Happiness goes to the
Stranger's head, and, believing himself a superman of the Nietzschean type and consequently
superior to everything, he challenges Heaven.
The Lady is shocked at his blasphemy and tells
him that he is like the idiot Cæsar.

The Stranger and the Lady wend their way to
her parents' house (i.e. Frida's parents). Their
condition is such that they are thought to be
beggars and have to eat in the kitchen. When the
Mother discovers their identity, she pours abuse on
the Stranger and accuses him of having tried to
destroy womankind. She forces the Lady, her
daughter, to read a terrible book (*The Confession
of a Fool*) which the Stranger has asked her to

avoid ; and, when the Lady learns of the Stranger's
first marriage, she turns from him in disgust and
becomes a scourge where before she had been kind
and helpful to him.

The Stranger recognises that he must go, and
in the next scene he is found in an institution to
which he has been taken. It is the fantasy of a
man in a delirium. People who have played a part
in his life are seated on one side of the table and
the Stranger sits solitary at the other. He has
owned up to the most heinous sins, and the
Confessor curses him. Unable to bear the curse,
the Stranger runs in search of the Lady, but finds
that she has gone to seek him. The Old Man is
dead and the Mother tells the Stranger that his
only hope of salvation is to retrace his steps and
do good where before he has done evil. After a
search, the Stranger and the Lady meet in the
mountain cottage, but now it is winter and both
are weighed down by the recognition of their sins.
They know they must live the past over again,
and they go back to the hotel room, to the
Werewolf, and then to the street corner from
which they had begun their wanderings.

The second part is also concerned with the
marriage of Strindberg and Frida. As she, in
Strindberg's opinion, had turned against him
because she did not wish to bear his child, so in
To Damascus the Lady becomes a tyrant as soon as
the Stranger's child is about to be born, pries into
his correspondence, makes him live in disgraceful

conditions, and talks of the child as being destined to revenge her on the Stranger. The Stranger's love is turned to hatred, and he leaves her. He goes to enjoy the fame of his scientific discoveries, and is given a banquet as the man who has succeeded in making gold. But the distinguished guests give place to the outcasts of society as soon as the Stranger rises to reply to the laudatory speeches, and, instead of receiving a scientific distinction, the Stranger is elected to the order of drunkards and left to pay the bill. The maker of gold cannot pay ! He is imprisoned, and on his release sinks lower and lower, yet fails to find anyone who is quite as low as himself. The Stranger creeps back to the Lady, but their lives cannot be joined together again, for they irritate and madden each other. The Lady has the solace of the child, but the Stranger has nothing. The Dominican (who is the same character as the Beggar) invites the Stranger to renounce the world, and the Stranger determines that there is no rest or happiness for him but in a monastery.

The third part of *To Damascus* was not written until six years later. Here the Stranger is revealed as in a mood of doubt. The Lady appears and tries to draw the Stranger back, but he rises superior to the love of women and is quite determined to adopt the monastic life. One last request he makes is that he should see his first wife (Siri), and this is granted. The Stranger discovers that she has not improved, while the eldest daughter of the marriage is a "new woman." The Stranger pauses no longer, but enters the monastery to find a lasting peace.

The public admission of his overbearing pride in seeking to penetrate the forbidden mysteries, of his sensuality, of his foolish imaginings, had to be written before Strindberg could turn to other work, and the writing of the first two parts of the drama relieved his mind. His next play, *Advent*, was called by Strindberg a "mystic legend" inspired by Swedenborg. It depicts a typical Swedenborgian hell, and introduces us to a judge and his wife who cannot bear the light to shine and shut out the sun whenever they can. They have always kept within the letter of the law, and feel safe in pursuing a wicked course since earthly justice takes no cognisance of such evil. *Crimes and Crimes*, which followed, also deals with the question of actions which are unpunished by man-made law but which are sins against heaven. Maurice, a young dramatist, triumphs with his first play in Paris and is encouraged by Henriette to wish for the death of the child of a liaison with a simple-minded woman. The child dies, and Maurice is accused of the murder. It is discovered, however, that death was due to natural causes. But Strindberg makes Maurice seek to atone since he has incurred a moral responsibility. In wishing the child out of the way, he has committed a crime that must be punished though earthly justice imposes no penalty. In these two

plays, published together under the title of *A
Higher Tribunal*, Strindberg indicates one stand-
point that he has adopted as a result of his experiences. He who had believed himself above morality was now the strictest of moralists. But that
did not restrain him, in *Crimes and Crimes*, from
portraying as Henriette the Norwegian Dagny
Juel who had married Prsybyszevski. In writing
the play, Strindberg may have had in mind the
occasion on which he had tried to harm his own
child in order to bring about a reconciliation
with Frida.

Seventeen years had passed since Strindberg had
written historical dramas. He had always been
keenly interested in historical movements, and felt
that he had in him the power to create works
which would set a new standard in the theatre.
The failure to obtain production for *Master Olof*
when first written had, however, induced him to
turn to other forms. Now he determined to come
back to his first love. *Master Olof* had been revived in 1897 and received with acclamation, and
Strindberg had again the ambition to give to
Sweden dramas worthy of his country's history.
He took Shakespeare as his model, and made a
close study of the plays themselves and of the best
commentaries on them. The first of the historical
dramas, *The Saga of the Folkungs*, shows very
clearly the influence of Shakespeare, and all of
them contain passages which it is easy to parallel
in Shakespeare. (In some of his plays, indeed,

Strindberg is not above direct plagiarism.)
Gustavus Vasa and *Eric XIV* were also written in
1899, and in the following year *Gustavus Adolphus*
and *Engelbrecht* were published.

Strindberg, who had carried simplification
almost to excess, now declared that he loved the
crowded stage, the rich apparel, the brilliant
scene, and that only in historical drama did he
feel quite at ease. He swung, however, from
extreme to extreme, and such a statement must
not be taken too seriously. He had always been
keenly interested in history, and possessed a
marvellous power of evoking the past ; he saw
history, not in the light of kings and queens, but
as a question of sociological and economic
movements. He had set out with the express
intention of doing for Sweden what Shakespeare
had done for England with historical drama. He
has at least given to Sweden a cycle of historical
plays of which any country may be proud and
which is unsurpassed in modern times. A study
of the historical dramas, with especial reference
to the influence on them of Shakespeare's plays,
has recently been published by Miss Joan Bulman
in *Strindberg and Shakespeare*.

After some months in Paris, Strindberg had
returned to Lund, but he was never happy to be
away from cities for long at a time, and he went
back to Stockholm as soon as he could raise
enough money. For the rest of his life he lived
in the Swedish capital, which he loved and knew

intimately. In the early days of his return he retained something of the look of a madman, and his eyes showed his inward disquiet. He could not bear to talk of the past years of misery, and regarded the world as conspiring to take advantage of him.

He had hoped to find a circle such as that which had met in the Red Room at Bern's twenty-five years ago, but the passage of time had changed his old friends. Strindberg felt himself a misfit, one doomed to solitude. He wanted to see his children, and was overjoyed when he was allowed to visit the second daughter of his first marriage. " Life does not seem so implacable as I believed," he writes to a friend after the visit ; but it was only a visit, and he hungered to have them always with him. His solitude was largely self-imposed. Friendship was offered to him, but he could not accommodate himself to others in any way and he liked to believe himself a martyr for whom society had no place. The furniture in the lodgings displeased him, but he would not buy anything of his own, " for not to possess things is freedom." He rarely saw the landlady and practically never spoke to her. Each morning he went for a quick walk and considered the work he had allotted for the day. He lived like a hermit, and sometimes thought that he had lost the power of speech through not using his voice. When the loneliness was too terrible to be borne, he would go into a tramcar just to be near other human beings.

But at other times he rejoiced in his solitary
state, because it helped him to develop his telepathic powers. By looking at people he could tell
whether they were sympathetic or unsympathetic
towards him. He met the same men and women
day after day but he did not attempt to speak to
them. Words were crude in comparison with the
delicate telepathic exchanges between them. All
their lives, all their thoughts, seemed to be
known to him. At night he sat in his darkened
room and looked into other houses, a spectator
who shared happiness and misfortune with the
neighbours to whom he had never spoken.

While he was in this state, Strindberg made the
acquaintance of Harriet Bosse, a Norwegian
actress, and her charm and beauty drew him
from his seclusion. Her name appears frequently
in his letters, and he refers to her as " the actress
of the new century " and praises her performance
as Puck in *A Midsummer Night's Dream*. He sent
her roses – " with thorns, of course, for there are
no others." It was for Harriet Bosse that he
wrote *Easter*, one of the most beautiful of his
plays and one which he himself ranked among his
best. His sister had been an inmate of an asylum
for a number of years, and Strindberg from his
own experience had an understanding and sympathy for those branded as mentally unstable.
Eleonora, whom the world called mad, is tenderly
and lovingly drawn. Her father had embezzled
money, and the principal creditor wanders to and

fro outside the window of the house seemingly on the point of bringing complete ruin to the family. From the asylum, to which she has been sent as insane, Eleonora returns to introduce brightness and love to the home : but on her arrival she appears likely only to bring added and deeper sorrows. She had gone into a shop and, in the absence of the shopkeeper, taken a flower, leaving the money in payment on the counter. The money is not found, and there is a hue and cry for the thief. But the dark clouds gather only to be dispersed by her love, and peace comes to the stricken family.

" Eleonora," Strindberg writes, " is she who suffers in place of others." No more poetic figure is to be found in Strindberg's plays. The condition of the hearts of the characters in the play affects even the weather, and *Easter* is a delicate study of the healing influence that love exerts on the troubled once they have broken down the wall of selfish pride that surrounds them. Strindberg admitted his debt to Maeterlinck and to Rudyard Kipling (*The Brushwood Boy*) in writing the play.

Harriet Bosse as Eleonora in *Easter* captured all Stockholm. The actress was flattered by the attentions paid to her by Strindberg, the most outstanding literary man of his day in Sweden, but she hesitated to accept his offer of marriage. He could be very charming when he liked, but there were tales of his excesses throughout Stockholm

and there were the painful records of his miserable previous unions.   After refusing once,
however, she decided that it was her duty to
bring about a reconciliation between Strindberg
and mankind, and with that view she agreed to
marry him.

The marriage took place on the 6th of May,
1901, after many difficulties of the kind which
Strindberg brought on himself through a false
idea of independence. The divorce with Frida
Uhl had not been carried out in due form, and he
and Harriet Bosse could not at first be married.
Strindberg's suggestion was that they should
proclaim their union outside a church and place
on the door a notice saying, " Since this Christian
church has not wished to open its doors to conse-
crate our love, we have ourselves, under the vast
Heaven and in the presence of Him who sees all,
sworn fidelity to each other, have exchanged
rings and sought the benediction of God on our
union as man and wife. Go, stranger, and follow
our example."

A happier note was shown in Strindberg's
works after the meeting with Harriet Bosse.
The Crown Bride proclaims the doctrine of " love
for everything living, great and small," and
Swanwhite, a fairy play, also makes love triumph
over all difficulties. But *The Dance of Death*,
published shortly afterwards, is the cruellest and
most gloomy of all Strindberg's plays.

The Dance of Death is in two parts. It recalls

the naturalism of *Comrades* and the other plays of that time, but outdoes them all in venom and morbidity. Here is no weak man facing an ingenious woman, as in *The Father*, but a man even more devilish than the fiendish woman who is his wife. Each has determined to kill the other, and neither has scruples of any kind. At the last the husband dies, but the wife does not triumph as she sees him drop. She remembers him as he had come to her in his youth and strength, and it is the ardent and generous lover whom she sees. " He was a good and noble man," says the wife ; and she realises that the life which she had hoped to enjoy when he was removed from her path can now never be. With his death, nothing is left to the wife. For hatred was her life.

Is

CHAPTER X

(1902–1912)

Third marriage – return of persecution mania – popularity in
Sweden – a vicious attack – telepathic intuition – purifying
the world – the Strindberg theatre – chamber plays – Fanny
Falkner – the Blue Tower – " the only truth."

AGAIN marriage was a failure. Difficulties soon
arose between Strindberg and Harriet Bosse, and
in 1902 the marriage state is once more arraigned
as an impossible burden for a man. *The Dream
Play*, written in this year, shows Strindberg to
have lost his faith in the power of love to triumph.
The fantasy presents love as a feeble support, and
Strindberg adopts a pessimistic view of unions
between men and women. The daughter of the
gods comes to earth, but finds only misery and
discontent. " Men are miserable creatures," is
her verdict as she finds that what on the surface
appears happiness is, when one digs deeper, only
suffering and disillusionment.

A child of the marriage, born in 1903, was not
the " bond " between them that Strindberg had
anticipated. Harriet had married him with the
idea of reconciling him to mankind, but that
seemed more than anyone could achieve with this
troubled man. Certainly she failed dismally in
this respect. " I must," he wrote to a friend,
" recover my liberty of thought and action,
without which a thinking man cannot exist." At

the end of 1904 they separated by mutual consent ;
but Strindberg still retained his admiration for
his wife's acting and saw her and his child peri-
odically. When they were parted, he could never
understand how the disagreements arose ; but
immediately he met Harriet the dissension broke
out again. Thus it had ever been with Strindberg.

His three marriages had been tragic failures.
He wanted the mother, living only for her home
and children, and on each occasion he married
a woman with outside interests – Siri and Harriet
were on the stage, Frida was a writer. His ideal
was the Swedish woman, yet he married a Finn,
an Austrian, and a Norwegian. But one can
hardly conceive any partner who could have
brought happiness for long to this quarrelsome
and suspicious soul. A wife, he said, learned to
know her husband's thoughts, and Strindberg
could not suffer anyone to read his mind.

He was again in the throes of persecution mania
after the separation from Harriet Bosse. Strange
noises prevented him from concentrating, books
fell without cause, his papers were found to be in
disarray. It appeared probable that Strindberg
would sink into madness once more, but through
the careful attention of the few friends whom he
permitted to visit him the crisis was averted. He
found solace in his historical studies, but for the
present he deserted the historical drama.

In *Gothic Rooms*, he returned to his attack on the

society of the nineties and aroused fierce resentment, but *Black Flags* was the book responsible for the harshest criticism, and deservedly so. Strindberg had been accepted by the public as the grand old man of Swedish literature and regarded as a privileged person. His brutal attacks were forgiven for the sake of the brilliance of the work he had given to the world and for his services to his country's literature. Popularity, which Strindberg had sought ardently, had come too late. He despised the critics who had not appreciated his genius in the early years and only joined in the chorus of praise because they dared not now go against the tide. The critics thought that he had forgotten how to bite and that he was harmless. Strindberg proved to them their mistake in *Black Flags*.

The novel, probably Strindberg's finest in some ways, has been described as the most libellous book in Swedish literature, and would be difficult to equal in any modern literature. It was a direct attack on Geijerstam, though other writers figure in it (Selma Lagerlöf is thinly disguised as Thelma Lagerlök). It was, however, aimed against Geijerstam, the man who for years had acted as his literary adviser and his agent in placing books and plays ; again and again in Strindberg's private correspondence reference is made to Geijerstam's services, and especially to his assistance in times of acute financial distress. Against this friend Strindberg now turned his

wrath, and knew no reserves in virulence. Strindberg believed that Geijerstam was partly responsible for the dissolution of the marriage with
Harriet Bosse, and that, presuming on the long
friendship, Geijerstam had taken liberties with
his work. Even if this had been entirely true,
Black Flags was a terrible revenge. Geijerstam
was depicted as a literary tout and swindler, and
dared not show himself in society after this vindictive attack ; he deserted his old haunts and
died shortly afterwards, a heart-broken man.

The book was more than the public could
excuse, even in " the grand old man." The
critics, who, as Strindberg suspected, had never
appreciated his work, rose in resentment against
this shameful attack, and Strindberg felt that he
had a grievance against them. He was shocked
at his own viciousness, and judged himself
severely for having written the book ; but he
did not admit the right of anyone to criticise
him, and he replied in a series of crushing re-
joinders. Years afterwards critics, who had forgotten what they had written about *Black Flags*,
found themselves assailed for their attacks on the
book. Strindberg had a long memory.

Not for the first time, Strindberg saw himself
as an outcast, bearing all the sins of the community
since a sacrifice of some kind must be found for
an erring world. That is the theme of *The
Scapegoat*. Libotz, the hero, goes to prison in
place of his drunken father, is robbed of his

fiancée, and from prosperity descends to bitter poverty. It is hard to see Strindberg in this gentle saint, but Strindberg meant Libotz to stand for himself. He believed, like Libotz, that he was purifying the world by taking upon himself the sins of others.

But Strindberg did not always consider himself as a man unjustly condemned and isolated. Sometimes he felt that he deserved to be cast out, and even that he was not suffering deeply enough. He demanded heavier and still heavier burdens to carry ; for a man of his strength, such trials were too easy – hardly worthy of him, in fact ! Now he would see in these sufferings an attempt to win him away from his faith in God, and consequently welcome the testing ; again he would rebelliously break out and engage in warfare with all whom he imagined to have inflicted the slightest injury on him. The shopkeepers were his enemies ; they seemed banded against him. Did he buy boots, they pinched his feet. Clothes never fitted him. The prices were always raised when he entered a shop.

His direct contacts with people became even fewer, but he had his world of telepathic intuition. When one of his plays was performed in a distant capital, he would hear the applause although it might be days later before the first news of the production came. He suffered the pains of childbirth when a woman in a neighbouring house was in labour, and he referred casually to having undergone numerous operations which had been performed on his friends, and even on strangers. Huysman's *En Route* – which appeared before *Inferno* and has much in common with it, although Strindberg denied the influence – probably affected him by the description of the monastic orders which bore the earthly pains of others. " I have twice gone through the death agony of others, with consequent physical and mental suffering," Strindberg says calmly. " The last time I passed through three diseases in six hours, and rose well when death had freed the absent one. This makes life painful, but rich and interesting."

Strindberg came out of his retirement to take a keen interest in the Intimate Theatre which August Falck, a young producer, had established in Stockholm. The theatre was intended to be experimental, and to offer a stage to all dramatists with new ideas who could not obtain a hearing in the commercial theatre, but it developed into a Strindberg Theatre. The stage was small, and elaborate productions were impossible ; but Strindberg, changing his mind once again, declared that all plays should be able to be presented before simple draperies. Footlights he abhorred as making for distortion, and they were abolished at his request. The theatre was modelled on the Little Theatres of Germany, and the innovations of Reinhardt and other advanced producers were adopted, with some typically Strindbergian modifications. In all things that related to the theatre,

Strindberg was an untiring enthusiast. He had appealed for a free theatre. " It may be necessary for the conventional laws to be broken," he said, " but let us have a theatre where everything is admitted except the talentless, the hypocritical, and the stupid." He was grateful to the actors and actresses and wrote sympathetically of the sufferings they endured night after night in playing painful parts, for Strindberg believed that the actor must feel the pangs of the character whom he represented.

It was in a spirit of revenge that Strindberg took control of the theatre. He intended to use it against society which had rejected him, and especially against the theatrical managers who had refused to play his work. In Paris, Berlin, Vienna, and elsewhere, Strindberg was staged ; in Stockholm the theatres refused to put on his masterpieces. But the rebellious mood was not always in evidence. Sometimes he approached his work in the theatre in a spirit of Christian humility, and saw himself as in duty bound to use the theatre to call upon the people to make their peace with God. The Christian humility, it may be mentioned, revealed itself most clearly in Strindberg when financial difficulties threatened the existence of the theatre.

In its early days the theatre was strikingly successful, and Strindberg was so delighted at having a stage on which he could depend for sympathetic interpretation of his plays that he wrote four pieces specially for production there. His intention was to carry into the drama the idea of chamber music, and he numbered his plays like musical compositions, Opus 1, Opus 2, etc. The plays, *Storm, The Burned House, The Ghost Sonata,* and *The Pelican,* are of unequal merit. Strindberg himself calls *Storm* " an excellent play for Philistines." In his *Kammerspel* he tries to show that things are not what they seem, and that only by bringing the hidden secrets into the light of day can the maladies be cured. " Every family has numerous secrets," he writes, " but men are too arrogant to admit it." Strindberg's intention to reveal the infamy that lurks behind a fair exterior was carried out with characteristic thoroughness. He explained that he avoided " brilliant rôles," and that he purposely omitted scenes and speeches which would have brought applause and for which the ordinary playwright would have sought.

If Ibsen borrowed from Strindberg for *Hedda Gabler,* Strindberg learned much from Ibsen for the chamber plays. *Storm,* the weakest of the four, reveals the loneliness that Strindberg felt after his parting from Harriet Bosse, though he makes his hero refuse to take back the erring wife. It was on his advice that Harriet had remarried, but he always hated to think that his child should be at the mercy of a stepfather, and *Storm* introduces such a situation. *The Burned House* deals with a home which to the world appeared happy

and respectable but which he strips of its coverings
to exhibit as a hell for children and a resort of vice.

The Ghost Sonata is the best of the four plays,
and one of the most extraordinary of all Strindberg's later plays. The vampire this time is in
male form and is inhuman enough to rank with
the vampire women of Strindberg's naturalistic
period. Hummel, the paralysed director of
eighty, who seeks revenge on those who have
injured him in the past and who tries to drain
others of life and vitality, takes the characters in
an apparently ordinary house and demonstrates
the sinfulness of their pasts. Ghosts come and go ;
the consul who is about to be buried appears in
his winding-sheet to see that the beggars to whom
he had given alms in his lifetime turn out in force
for the funeral ; a milkmaid, symbol of Hummel's
past wrongdoing, is seen by him and him only ;
a woman has become mummified and is half dead,
half alive ; for her sins, she spends her life in a
cupboard and cries out like a parrot. But she
emerges from her prison to recall the crime of
Hummel and force him to kill himself.

The Pelican is entitled so ironically. For the
mother of the play lives at the expense of her
children in order to get money for her lover.
Again Strindberg unveils the secrets of a household so deeply lost in sin that the house and all in
it must die. In this piece Strindberg returns to a
theme that is found elsewhere : that the people
who cook the food can take the goodness out of it

before serving. He suggests that servants do so, and thus starve their masters and mistresses. That is the revenge they take for having to be subservient !

The Strindberg Theatre, after its brilliant start, got into debt. Strindberg offered all his property – he never in the course of his whole life had much – and his books as guarantee for a loan. The theatre was saved and Strindberg felt that another attack of his enemies had been defeated. But the respite was only temporary, and debts accumulated to such an extent that the theatre had to be sold. Strindberg felt its loss keenly. To Falck and the others who had helped him in putting his ideas before the public, Strindberg turned from an admiring friend into an implacable and voluble enemy. He suspected that they had purposely tried to ruin the theatre so that it should pass out of his control. He dubbed them his betrayers.

One of the actresses he had met at the theatre, Fanny Falkner, revived Strindberg's dreams of achieving happiness in marriage. She lived with her mother in the Blue Tower, to which Strindberg moved and where he spent the remaining years of his life. The Falkners took their duties towards him seriously, and, so far as creature comfort was concerned, Strindberg was more happy than ever before. Miss Falkner has told the story of those last years in *Strindberg i bla tornet* (*Strindberg in the Blue Tower*). She was engaged to Strindberg, but only for a short time. Miss Falkner had evidence of his peculiar manners, his violence, his dealings with the friendly and unfriendly " powers," and she decided that life with him was an ordeal that she could not face.

Strindberg expressed himself heartbroken. After a period of silence, he engaged in another literary outburst, full of rancour against a world which had combined to refuse him a fourth wife. *The Great Highway*, not one of his best works, again presents Strindberg as a much burdened, much persecuted man. It was the last of his plays. He wrote as furiously as ever during the remaining two years of his life, but he had finished with the theatre. His principal work was the preparation of *The Blue Books*, a remarkable series of dialogues in which, in the form of question and answer, the Teacher and the Pupil discuss life in its various manifestations. There are few subjects which fail to receive mention in the four volumes of *The Blue Books*, which Strindberg called " the synthesis of my life," and for which he had been preparing for years.

In 1910 he was offered a column in a newspaper, and he accepted the opportunity to discourse to the Swedish people on how to live. The brilliance of his writing and the wisdom of his articles won back for Strindberg the respect of his countrymen that had been lost by *Black Flags* and other vindictive thrusts. Honours were offered to him, but he refused them all, sometimes calling the

distinctions worthless, at other times professing
himself guilty of such unpardonable crimes that
he was unfit to accept any honour. The Nobel
Prize was never to be his. He had sneered at the
prize, and there was a long-standing feud between
him and the then secretary, who had a voice in
the choice of recipients. A fund to which all
classes subscribed was raised for Strindberg, but
he would only accept it as an " anti-Nobel Prize."
He gave the money to charity and to causes in
which he was interested.

On the 22nd of January, 1912, his sixty-third
birthday was celebrated as a national event.
Special performances of his plays were given
throughout Sweden, processions filed past the
Blue Tower in Stockholm to acclaim their foremost writer. Strindberg insisted on acknowledg-
ing the homage of the people, though he was ill at
the time. After the beginning of 1912 he had
known himself for a doomed man. Cancer of the
stomach was discovered, and an operation failed
to arrest the disease. He suffered acutely for
several months, but insisted on writing his notes
for *The Blue Books* and his daily newspaper
article.

He died on the 14th of May with the Bible
clasped close to his breast. " This," he said,
pointing to the Bible, " is the only truth." The
funeral took place in the early morning air which
he had loved, and sixty thousand people came to
pay their last tribute. Every class and profession

were represented ; the rich and the poor, the learned societies, the students' clubs, the working men's associations mingled together. Strindberg was buried neither among the aristocrats nor among the plebeians. He had asked that he should lie alone, and his resting-place is at the top of a hill under firs. In this tortured soul Sweden lost no lovable man, but in August Strindberg she mourned her greatest writer and a mighty force in European literature.

His influence on the Continent has been considerable, and in France and Germany – and of course in his own country – much has been written of his services to the drama and the novel. His work was introduced into England at the beginning of the century, and had a minor boom. The name of Strindberg is again becoming known here. When the Nobel Prize for Literature was awarded to Mr. George Bernard Shaw, he devoted the money to a scheme for making Swedish masterpieces available in translation, and naturally the Anglo-Swedish Literary Foundation began its work by the publication of Strindberg's plays. (It is ironical that Strindberg, who ridiculed the Nobel Prize, should owe a translation of his work to the money provided by that prize.) In 1933 a Scandinavian Theatre was established in London for the production of plays by Scandinavian dramatists, and chose for its first two productions Strindberg's *The Dream Play* and *Easter.*

Strindberg may never have another boom in England, but masterpieces such as his do not pass away. In his life he was brutal and vindictive, full of rancour and bitterness, occasionally foolish and sometimes vicious ; and twenty years after his death we need not forget that often he was trying to revenge the injustices that he believed the world had done him. We remember that if Strindberg inflicted suffering on others, he also suffered deeply himself, and that in face of many difficulties he achieved greatly. When a child, he told a religious woman that he would " rather be a genius than one of God's chosen." No one will doubt the genius of August Strindberg.

BIBLIOGRAPHY

THE main source is Strindberg's autobiography, but no complete translation is at present available in English.

Miss Lind-af-Hageby, who knew Strindberg in Stockholm, has written an interesting study in *August Strindberg*, and an American writer, W. J. McGill, has recently published a biography under the title, *August Strindberg, the Bedeviled Viking*.

Le Théâtre de Strindberg, by A. Jolivet, is an excellent study of Strindberg's contribution to the European stage. There are several good biographies in German, of which *August Strindberg, Die Geschichte einer kämpfenden und leidenden Seele*, by Nils Erdmann, and *August Strindberg im lichte seines Lebens und seiner Werke*, by Herman Esswein, can be strongly recommended.

For a study of Strindberg's mental crisis see *Strindberg und Van Gogh*, by Karl Jaspers, and for the correspondence between Nietzsche and Strindberg see *Nietzsche und Strindberg*, by Karl Strecker.